# The German Army and Genocide

# The German Army and Genocide

Crimes Against War Prisoners, Jews, and Other Civilians in the East, 1939–1944

Edited by the Hamburg Institute for Social Research

Translated from the German by Scott Abbott with editorial oversight by Paula Bradish and the Hamburg Institute for Social Research

The New Press, New York, 1999

Conception, research, and texts:
Dr. Bernd Boll
Hannes Heer
Dr. Walter Manoschek
Christian Reuther
Dr. Hans Safrian

Director, research project and exhibition:
Hannes Heer

Visual conception and design:
Christian Reuther
Johannes Bacher

First published as *Vernichtungskrieg. Verbrechen der Wehrmacht 1941 bis 1944*
Published in the United States by The New Press, New York
Distributed by W. W. Norton & Company, Inc., New York

The publisher is grateful to the Indiana University Press for permission
to reprint a portion of Omer Bartov's "German Soliders and the Holocaust,"
from *History and Memory*, Volume 9, Numbers 1/2 (Fall 1997).
© Indiana University Press, 1997.

ISBN 1-56584-525-0

The New Press was established in 1990 as a not-for-profit alternative
to the large, commercial publishing houses currently dominating
the book publishing industry. The New Press operates in the public interest
rather than for private gain, and is committed to publishing, in innovative ways,
works of educational, cultural, and community value that are often deemed
insufficiently profitable.

www.thenewpress.com

Printed in the United States of America

9 8 7 6 5 4 3 2 1

# Contents

Michael Geyer  Foreword

The exhibition *The Germany Army and Genocide* is a German contribution to the fiftieth anniversary of the end of World War II. When it opened in Hamburg in March 1995, it unleashed a storm that would not subside. Public interest was quite unlike anything Germany and, for that matter, Austria had seen before, although this was surely not the first national debate on the Nazi past. The exhibition elicited a shock of recognition. As it toured from city to city, it had the effect of a national purgatory.

By 1995, the times when the Germans did not care to know about the Nazi past were gone. The exhibition was but one effort among many to call forth the horrors of Nazi genocide for which the Germans had found one of those seemingly endless words which give the matter a certain gravity: *Vergangenheitsbewältigung* or the coming-to-terms-with-the-past. But for all the acknowledgment of a murderous past, knowing the past as history is one thing.

Encountering or experiencing oneself in the past is an entirely different matter. Surprisingly, this is what happened wherever the exhibition was shown.

Recognition was above all a matter of literally seeing oneself or one's own in the images displayed. Visitors discovered themselves or their relatives in the photographs of the *Wehrmacht* exhibition, remembered having seen similar scenes or, if they were somewhat younger, having seen similar photographs at home. There was also a metaphorical act of recognition when a post-postwar generation—those who were about the age of the people portrayed in the photographs and had grown up in a very different world—wondered what they, put into the same situation, would have done. Young and old may well have preferred to identify with the victims as they had done on other occasions. But here they recognized themselves as killers of unarmed men, women, and children.

The exhibition differs from many efforts that elicit the horrors of the Nazi past and of World War II in that it focuses, not on the apparatus of extermination, but on the *Wehrmacht*. The *Wehrmacht* was the institution where all young German men did their military service. About twenty million men were in service during World War II, to whom one would have to add a fair number of women in auxiliary services. Exemptions were rare. Whatever may be said about the involuntary nature of service in some elements of the SS or in police regiments, the *Wehrmacht* was where German men experienced and fought war.

But it is not just the numbers. The *Wehrmacht* was a popular institution, even though soldiers did not necessarily like the army. It was, above all, a representative institution because the *Wehrmacht* was above a certain age. *Wehrmacht* lore, in turn, articulated the experience, the hopes and expectations, of a generation of German men who had survived the war and built postwar Germany. After the war, the *Wehrmacht* became every man's bill to a clean conscience. For the *Wehrmacht* was the millions of good people as opposed to the bad hundred-thousands in the SS that acknowledge the burden of the German past—or so it was thought.

This is where the exhibition exploded a fantasy. To be sure, there had always been a sense that "bad things happened in Russia" and nothing good was expected to come out of Serbia. This general and quite prejudicial sentiment thickened into something of a self-critical consensus, although not without a fight, after the meticulous official historians of the German Military History Research Office had demonstrated, on the basis of vast archival material, the systematic nature of the violation of the law of war on the part of the *Wehrmacht* and, more hesitantly, on the part of the ordinary soldier. They spoke of an ideological war that Hitler unleashed with the willing complicity of the higher military echelons.

Yet putting this argument into visible evidence sent tremors through Germany and Austria. The war "in the East" was not simply a particularly ruthless, ideologically charged war, but it now appeared as a destructive war against entire populations— a war which aimed at the total annihilation of some groups of people and the decimation and enslavement of others. The occupation of Poland was now seen as a laboratory and the anti-partisan war in Serbia as the testing ground for a deliberate politics of ethnic cleansing, colonization, and enslavement. In its destructive and exterminist drive, the war of the *Wehrmacht* was deliberate and self-generated—a reflection, in the first instance, of German wants and fears rather than enemy actions. These wants and fears can best be summarized as, respectively, a shared sense of German superiority and the imagined bestiality of the enemy.

The war that is documented in this exhibition is a war of annihilation. This is to say, first, that this war was fought against entire peoples rather than against their armies and their war industries. Entire peoples became disposable, designed to be disposed of after conquest. Second, as an effect of highest level orders, certain enemy populations, such as Jews and Commissars, were marked for outright annihilation. This is what we see in the exhibition: War appears as the taking and killing of hostages as was the case in Serbia; the slaughter of Jews in Babi Yar; the mass hangings from balconies in Kharkow; the starvation of Russian prisoners of war; the enslavement of men, women, and children in the form of forced laborers, as household servants and as prostitutes. It is a war without a front. To be sure, this is not the entire war, but it is an essential segment of it.

Since the *Wehrmacht* was a genuine people's army this war of utter destruction and enslavement of civilian populations was the war that the German people fought. The shock came with the fact that this was an exhibition about (potentially) every man and, somewhat at the margins of many images but clearly present, of every woman. It was not necessarily what these men and women liked—and even less what they liked to be remembered for. But it was what they did. The real difference of this exhibition comes with the recognition that this war was put into practice not by generals but by people like you and me or, in any case, by Germans like you and me.

Saying this or writing it down is one thing; it is, in any case, something to be debated. But seeing it and seeing it having been photographed is a somewhat different matter. The power of the many, small, mostly ama-

teur photographs, which make up the major evidence of the exhibition, is overwhelming. Here were soldiers photographing without the least compunction other soldiers committing atrocities. The absence of a sense of guilt or shame, the absence of any second thought (not among all, but among many)—this is almost harder to take than the dissolution of the boundary between military and criminal conduct, between civility and barbarity.

To have first-hand testimony, in the form of hundreds and hundreds of photographs, of a moral blindness that afforded men (and the occasional woman) to see repugnant acts without recognizing them as such—this is a challenge to what we fervently wish to hold self-evidently true: that human beings are capable of distinguishing between right and wrong. It is this profound disablement of moral judgement that took aback those who saw the exhibition in Germany and Austria.

The moving effect of the exhibition in Germany and Austria was that Germans like you and me stopped, looked, and began to see. Often they disagreed about the representative nature of these images and some members of the older generation as well as some of the very young disagreed violently. But while the majority may not have literally recognized themselves, they did see what they had not seen in 1939-1945 or what subsequent generations had somehow accepted in the abstract but never quite imagined as a tangible reality and challenge to their own moral judgement. They now saw people being put to death. They came in order to see.

What is there to see once the exhibition crosses the borders from the German-into the English-speaking world? What will those in the United States and Canada, viewing the photographic traces of a former enemy whom they defeated, but never encountered as a deadly force on their own territory see?

There are, I think, a few things to bear in mind. The war that is exhibited here is not the one of North Africa, Anzio, the beaches of Normandy, or the crossing of the Rhine. This is the war beyond the American and

English theaters of war, but as far as the German *Wehrmacht* is concerned it was the main war. Thirteen out of twenty million German soldiers fought or served "in the East" at one point or another. The main theater of war in what Eric Hobsbawm has called the "age of extremes" is to the east of Germany, not to the west. This war—unleashed in the attack on Poland, fought with relentless violence in Serbia, and culminating in the war against Russia—devastated Europe in the twentieth century.

The victims of this war are not often encountered in the North American context because, after the defeat of Nazi Germany, they became the enemies of the West almost instantly. This was a war of enslavement foremost against Poles and Russians; it was a ruthless war of subjugation and occupation against Serbians (and, for that matter, against Greeks). As such it was a war of utter destruction, of total disregard for the life and property of each and everyone. It seems that, in reflection and hindsight, this may well appear to be an apt subject for contemplation on this side of the Atlantic. However, this theater of war is beyond the American imagination, even if not beyond the ethnic memory of quite a significant group of North Americans. It requires learning to see through the eyes of others.

Against the stark background of the war of annihilation in eastern Europe and Russia that the exhibition evokes the mark of the Holocaust becomes more clearly visible. This mark is not to be found in the savagery of destruction. Atrocities have a certain universal characteristic of dehumanization. Hence, lingering over acts of atrocity, although horrendous, will not make evident what happened to Jews in Nazi occupied Europe. However, the deliberate identification of Jews as a separate group even among outcasts, such as the Soviet prisoners of war, does make a difference. In a cruel politics of difference Jews were marked for death rather than being an expendable population. The killing of Jews, the extermination of any and all, was separated out from the general violence of decimation and enslavement.

Nonetheless, the marking of Jews, as a population branded for death, cannot be separated from the savagery of the war in eastern and southeastern Europe. As the images indicate and the text of this exhibition suggests, the war of annihilation and the war of extermination were both subject to military consideration. Highest level military orders identified Jews as particularly dangerous enemies in what was to be a savage war. From all we know, soldiers seemed to concur. A look at the evidence on Serbia may serve as a chilling reminder of how tightly military necessity, anti-semitism, and anti-slavic racism were imbricated.

How this happened and why the *Wehrmacht*, although not the major actor in the campaign of extermination against the Jews, got so deeply entangled in extermination is a subject well worth further inquiry. As we see German soldiers engaged in heinous and repugnant acts of slaughter, we recognize that this inquiry will have to encompass the issue of normalcy and civility in their relation to savagery and cruelty. For it is one of the most disturbing features of these photographs that they neither show cartoon stereotypes of vicious and sadistic brutes nor haughty officers and SS supermen. These soldiers are people quite unlike anything movies, television, and quite a few books would like to make us believe. They look in uniform much like what they would become in postwar life—your average Fritz, Franz or Otto. They look perfectly normal, but committed extraordinary atrocities. We would not recognize them for what they did—were it not for the photographs that depict what they did, but did not see for themselves, until years later.

In learning to see what these ordinary men in *Wehrmacht* uniform did not see, we discover that moral judgement is a cognitive ability—a process of learning to see what others have not seen and did not care to see. Some might want to use this insight in order to count the blessings of living in different times and different places. Others might recognize in this inability to see the corruption of civil norms and the blindness of perception that struck a nation which thought of itself as representing the very standards of civilization and that tarnished an army which thought of its valor as second to none. The ancient Greeks knew one or two things about humanity when they held that attitude, above all, was the beginning of disaster.

Note
*Wehrmacht* is the term used from 1935 to 1945 to refer to the German armed forces, comprising the land (Heer or army), sea (Marine or navy) and air force (Luftwaffe or airforce).

Omer Bartov Preface

## Professional Soldiers

Until the late 1960s the German *Wehrmacht* was generally presented in Germany and in much of the rest of the world as a professional organization that had fought a host of enemies with remarkable tenacity and skill and had little in common with the ideological world view and criminal policies of the Nazi regime. This view was disseminated by *Wehrmacht* veterans in postwar publications such as military formation chronicles and former generals' memoirs, just as much as in popular fiction and film; it was also the official line of the West German government.[1] German scholars rarely challenged the notion of the *Wehrmacht's* "purity of arms" even as they

gradually shifted toward a positive evaluation of the military-conservative opposition that had attempted to overthrow Hitler, allegedly due to the threat he posed to the army's "shield of honor," and more obviously because of the looming defeat by the Allies whose anticipated catastrophic consequences might have been somewhat diminished by doing away with the Nazi leadership.[2] Western scholars generally accepted this view, not least because their perspective of the war was based on the manner in which it was fought in the West, where, with the possible exception of the very last months of the fighting, both sides adhered to some conventions of warfare that had long disappeared under torrents of blood and material devastation in the East.[3]

The German soldier's presentation as a professional fighter, untouched by or uninvolved in the crimes of the regime, was of course directly related to the context of domestic and international political circumstances immediately following the end of the war. Domestically, it seemed impossible to rebuild West German society without as narrow as possible a definition of the so-called Nazis and their accomplices.[4] The idea that the *Wehrmacht* as such might have been a criminal organization was not only anathema to German public opinion but would have implicated such vast portions of German society in Nazi criminality that one would have had either to declare a general amnesty (thereby legitimizing the notion of unpunished crimes) or to give up altogether the possibility of resurrecting some form of a German national entity. Considering that as many as twenty million Germans had passed through the ranks of the *Wehrmacht* at one point or another, neither of these options was realistic, especially in the face of a perceived Soviet threat and the rapid deterioration of international relations that swiftly led to the Cold War. Not only was it unthinkable to eliminate Germany as a nation, it was also

quickly transpired that the hopes and expectations of some Nazi leaders and *Wehrmacht* generals in the last phases of the war, namely that Germany would be a crucial factor in a Western anti-Communist alliance, were to be realized within a few years after the collapse of the Third Reich.[5]

The Nuremberg Trials and the attempted denazification of postwar Germany eventually served precisely this end, since in both cases the criminality of the regime and the extent of participation in crimes of war and genocide were defined in a manner that made possible the quick reemergence of the German state and society as somehow purged of the misdeeds of the past.[6] If the initial purpose had been to punish and purge, the ultimate result was to acquit and cover up. One should point out that this was not merely a consequence of either the inability to imagine the horror of genocide and find the appropriate legal discourse for it or of cold political calculations; it also manifested the sheer meaninglessness of indicting a whole nation and therefore served to demonstrate humanity's incapacity to confront the crime of modern genocide in a manner compatible with its scale and enormity and

the range of agencies, professions, and individuals that must perforce be complicit in it. Since 1945 we have witnessed many more cases of genocide whose makers were eventually welcomed back into the community of nations, not least because the evil they committed could never find appropriate retribution.[7]

It should also be noted that the state of knowledge regarding the army's involvement in Nazi crimes was not a function of any substantial lack in archival sources. Large quantities of German documents were taken to Britain and the United States after the war and later returned to Germany; much of the material eventually used by scholars had been available long before it was examined. What was lacking in those first two decades was scholarly interest, not evidence, as well as the more obvious limitations imposed on research by the vast amounts of material and the laborious process of its organization and categorization. At least as crucial, however, was the impact of certain interpretive concepts of Nazism specifically and methodological conventions about historical research more generally. This meant that during the reign of the paradigms of totalitarianism and fascism, scholars were often more interested in theory than in fact, and that with the emergence of social history, historians devoted little attention to the military.[8] Consequently, the only scholars to examine army records were so-called "pure" military historians, whose interests lay more in tactics and strategy, command and logistics, than in ideology and criminality. Mainstream historians therefore tended to rely mainly on the memoirs of German generals and veterans' accounts for the reconstruction of the soldiers' experience in the war. And precisely because former soldiers understandably stressed their professionalism and denied any ideological or organizational links with the regime, they were viewed as objective and reliable sources. It took a generation of scholars more skeptical about the explanatory power of the old paradigms, less trustful of former soldiers and, not least, willing to undermine the myths on which West German society was founded, to finally venture into the archives and begin to write the history of the *Wehrmacht* relationship with the Nazi regime.

Ideological Soldiers

German scholars such as Gerhard Ritter and Friedrich Meinecke, former *Wehrmacht* generals such as Heinz Guderian and Erich von Manstein, as well as Western military historians and former officers such as B. H. Liddell Hart and J. F. C. Fuller, and scholars such as Gordon Craig and John Wheeler-Bennett all stressed the vast distance between the "old" officer corps and the upstart Nazis and found it unthinkable that such respectable and "correct," if perhaps conservative and even reactionary, officers and gentlemen could have condoned, let alone organized, a criminal war and unprecedented genocide.[9] There were, to be sure, some rotten apples, who were justly condemned at Nuremberg; but by and large, it was argued, they were unrepresentative of the whole. Soviet claims that the *Wehrmacht* had engaged in genocidal war in the East were—with some reason—dismissed as communist propaganda. Western generals by and large preferred to think

of the war they had fought as chivalrous, and of the enemy as worthy of the fight. And military historians, as indeed much of the public, were more interested in the heroic exploits encapsulated in such popular novels and films as *The Longest Day* or *A Bridge Too Far* than in the horrors of genocidal war.

All this began to change thanks in large part to the efforts of a few outstanding and courageous German scholars, some of whom belonged to an important German research institute closely linked to the West German Ministry of the Interior and the Bundeswehr, which eventually produced a massive study, as yet still uncompleted, of the *Wehrmacht* in World War II.[10] Complemented by works written outside of Germany, this important body of literature is thus the outcome of a joint, and often contentious and controversial, effort by historians of several nations working over a span of some three decades who have, by the early 1990s, succeeded in drastically changing our understanding of the *Wehrmacht*'s role in the Third Reich.

The publication in 1965 of the two-volume work *Anatomie des SS-Staates*, which included an important analysis by Hans-Adolf Jacobsen of the so-called Commissar Order (the instruction to kill on the spot all political officers attached to Red Army units captured by the *Wehrmacht*), heralded the beginning of scholarly writings on the criminal activities of the *Wehrmacht* during its campaign in the Soviet Union.[11] This was followed in 1969 by a comprehensive study of the policies of ideological indoctrination in the *Wehrmacht* written by Manfred Messerschmidt, a path-breaking work on the maltreatment and murder of Soviet prisoners of war by Christian Streit, published in 1978, and a thorough investigation of the collaboration between the *Einsatzgruppen*, the death squads of the SS and SD, and the *Wehrmacht* by Helmut Krausnick and Hans-Heinrich Wilhelm, which appeared in 1981.[12] Along with several other studies such as Volker Berghahn's comprehensive article on "educational officers" and Klaus-Jürgen Müller's analysis of the army's relationship

with the Nazi state, these works established a new standard for the examination of the role of the *Wehrmacht* in the planning and execution of Hitler's policies in the East.[13] Moreover, since 1979 the Militärgeschichtliches Forschungsamt (Institute for Military History) in Freiburg (recently moved to Potsdam) has been publishing a massive series of volumes on the Third Reich and World War II. These tomes, and especially Volume 4 published in 1983, written by such leading German scholars in the field as Jürgen Förster, Bernhard Kroener, Rolf-Dieter Müller, Wilhelm Deist and Gerd Ueberschär, have vastly expanded our knowledge of the *Wehrmacht* and its links with the regime's policies.[14] Put together, this literature has had a major and lasting effect on the scholarship on the Third Reich and has become a sine qua non for any future research on the period, superseding older works by non-German scholars such as Alexander Dallin and Robert O'Neill.[15] The enormous archival ground work on which these studies were based swept aside many of the conventional assumptions on the *Wehrmacht*. Among them, and most important to the present context, was the idea of the army's professionalism and ideological detachment.

What the works cited here demonstrated was that, contrary to previous assertions, the *Wehrmacht* had come under the influence of the regime from very early on and remained a major tool in the implementation of Nazi policies until the very end of the war. This was expressed in the *Wehrmacht* command's willingness, if not eagerness, to subject the troops to substantial ideological training; in its participation in the planning and brutal execution of conquest and occupation on a vast scale; and in its central role in doing away with conventional rules and regulations of warfare, all of which deeply implicated it in the war of destruction and subjugation conducted by Germany in Eastern Europe and the Soviet Union. Such revelations, though anchored in a mass of documentation, were not immediately or easily accepted in Germany. Indeed, one characteristic of these publications was that they were repeatedly greeted in the media and by the public with expressions of astonishment and disbelief, horror and rage. As even some of the most recent debates on the *Wehrmacht*, to be discussed below, have indicated, the views expressed by these historians are still encountering a great deal of public resistance, although by now most scholars tend to accept them. The political impact of these works is of course immense, since they not only call for a profound reevaluation of the meaning and implications of the Nazi regime for German society during and after the war, they also discredit some of the most dearly held assumptions on the ability of postwar Germany to "come to terms" with its past.

Nevertheless, this body of scholarship suffers from several serious limitations. Employing a rather traditional methodology, these historians have mainly focused on the upper echelons of the military and the regime, have emphasized matters of higher policy and decision making and have shown a distinct reluctance to identify the links between the penetration of Nazi ideology into the *Wehrmacht*, its criminal conduct vis-à-vis the local population and enemy soldiers especially in the East, and the planning and implementation of the Holocaust. As will be noted in the next section, the connections between the *Wehrmacht* and the genocide of the Jews have only recently begun to receive appropriate scrutiny by historians. For the moment, however, let me first discuss a few more studies, mainly by non-German scholars, which have complemented and enriched the existing scholarship by concentrating on a "view from below" of the *Wehrmacht*, that is, on the manner in which the rank and file of the army behaved during the war, were influenced by the ideology of the regime and the views of their immediate superiors, and ultimately perceived their own actions at the front.

Studies of soldiers, rather than generals, were motivated both by developments in historical research and by the increasingly obvious limited of earlier work on the *Wehrmacht*. The new trend among historians in the 1970s and 1980s to "lower their gaze" and examine the everyday lives of "ordinary" people, rather than focus on either high politics or anonymous structures and mechanisms, was reflected in attempts to write an "Alltagsgeschichte" of the *Wehrmacht* somewhat akin to works being written at the time on German civilian society.[16] Similarly, the spate of "local histories" that strove to gain more insight into social and political changes by focusing in depth on a limited community was reflected in studies of discrete military units.[17] At the same time these studies tried to test the assertions of scholars writing about the top echelons, according to which the efforts to indoctrinate the troops were largely unsuccessful and the criminal orders issued by the high command rarely reached the units on the ground. Ironically, therefore, the very same historians who had documented the involvement of the *Wehrmacht* in Nazi policies were unwilling to go so far as to concede that the soldiers were actually influenced by their generals' decision to implement the policies of conquest and genocide dictated by the regime and to legitimize them by employing Nazi ideological arguments. Instead, they assumed that the troops were far more preoccupied with their own survival and accepted at face value the apologetic postwar argument by field commanders that they had refused to hand down to the soldiers such orders as the Kommissarbëfehl of which they claimed to have strongly disapproved.[18] Thus the new studies that focused on the lower echelons were consciously aimed at investigating the extent to which the troops were both influenced by ideological arguments and received and carried out the criminal orders of the regime and the army high command.

Works in this vein began appearing in the mid-1980s, but more than ten years later one can say that there is still a great deal of research to be done in this area. Earlier works by Theo Schulte and myself have more recently been followed by Stephen Fritz's and Thomas Kühne's studies.[19] Despite the rather meager scholarship on the everyday life of the troops, these scholars both tend to debate each other's conclusions and have met with a fair amount of criticism from other quarters.

Nevertheless, some of the more fundamental findings of these studies seem to have gained acceptance within the larger academic community. Among those most relevant to the present context is, first, that the soldiers were indeed exposed to a massive indoctrinational effort by the military authorities. Second, that especially as regards ideological teachings that had already been disseminated among German youth prior to their conscription in school, the Hitler Youth and the Labor Service, and which corresponded to preexisting prejudices in German society, the concerted propaganda aimed at the troops was largely successful in molding the men's views on the supreme quality of their political leadership, the inhuman character of the enemy, the ruthless manner in which fighting should be conducted, and the catastrophic consequences of defeat. Third, that under the combined influence of a dehumanizing ideology and a brutal war the troops of the *Wehrmacht* were involved in widespread crimes against enemy soldiers and the civilian population, acting both on orders by their superiors and in many instances also on their own initiative, even when such actions were explicitly forbidden by their commanders. All these factors put together led to what I have called the "barbarization of warfare" on the Eastern Front which resulted in the devastation of vast tracts of land, especially in the occupied parts of the Soviet Union, and caused the deaths of millions of civilians and POWs whether by outright murder or from starvation, epidemics, exposure to the elements and economic exploitation. In other words, both from the perspective of the generals and from that of the troops on the ground, the campaign in the East was conducted as a war of annihilation.

Taken as a whole, the scholarly study of the *Wehrmacht* and its relationship with the Third Reich, Nazi ideology and the policies of conquest, subjugation and annihilation pursued by the regime has made major strides in the past thirty years. However, one crucial area has been sorely neglected until very recently, namely, the role of the army in the genocide of the Jews. This was partly caused by disciplinary compartmentalization, whereby military historians studied issues deemed relevant to war and occupation, to which genocide did not seem to belong, while historians of the Holocaust refrained from studying the *Wehrmacht* and focused either on the agencies directly involved in organizing genocide or on the victims. Partly, this was a result of ideological and national biases, which in the German case meant that one found it exceedingly difficult to associate the *Wehrmacht*—for a long time after the war seen as the organization least contaminated by the Nazis and most representative of the common folk—with the Holocaust—recognized as the very worst of the many crimes committed by the Third Reich. Still another reason for this neglect was the realization of the implications that the potential findings of such research would have for the understanding of postwar German society, let alone for the many veterans and their relatives whose numbers have begun dwindling only in recent years. If the argument that the *Wehrmacht's* soldiers were involved in war crimes was already explosive and has indeed met with a great deal of resistance in Germany, associating the army with the Holocaust is far more disturbing. After all, the argument could have, and indeed has, been made that there was nothing unique about the involvement of German troops in wanton destruction, looting, exploitation and murder; war is hell, and nothing better could be expected of soldiers fighting in such terrible conditions as on the Eastern Front. The fact is that even those who rejected this position, such as myself, have written on the barbarization of warfare from the perspective of the troops and within the context of a horrendous war, which somehow made the narrative more palatable by making for a certain empathy with the soldiers themselves. The Holocaust, however, has commonly been presented as separate from the war (even if genocide on this scale could only have been practiced within its context), and its perpetrators were seen as separate from the soldiers. Associating the two therefore threatens to undermine the

last defensive barrier of the *Wehrmacht's* remarkably solid postwar fortifications. Precisely because in Germany the Holocaust was seen as the epitome of evil, it had to be ascribed to perpetrators kept rigidly apart from the rest of the population; linking it with the *Wehrmacht* therefore opens the floodgates and erases all distinctions, for the army included (virtually) everyone, and the survivors of the war became the founders of the two postwar Germanys. No wonder that this has always been perceived as a most threatening exercise.

Genocidal Soldiers

In the mid-1980s, just a few years before reunification, the German academic community and much of the more respectable media were shaken by a controversy over the uniqueness of the Holocaust and the manner in which the history of the Nazi regime should be contextualized in the creation of a new German national identity.[20] The *Historikerstreit*, as it came to be called, is relevant to the present discussion for two main reasons. First, because it concerned the effort by some German scholars to "normalize" the single most horrible undertaking of the Third Reich, the Holocaust, by linking it to other cases of genocide carried out by other states at other times in history. Second, because it included an attempt to present the German army's war in the East as a desperate struggle against an invading Bolshevik-Asiatic enemy who threatened to destroy not only Germany but the rest of Western civilization.[21] Hence the "revisionists" of the *Historikerstreit* were interested neither in denying the Holocaust nor in refuting claims about the barbarous manner in which the war in the East was conducted by the *Wehrmacht*, but rather in relativizing them both as "unoriginal" and as "necessary" because genocide had been originated by the very same regime whose alleged genocidal intentions had made fighting a barbarous war necessary, namely, the Bolsheviks.

As several critics of the historians' controversy noted at the time, the *Historikerstreit* introduced no new evidence, nor any original

interpretations, but was a political and ideological debate over the sense and meaning of the past and the manner in which it should (be allowed to) influence the present.[22] In one sense, it was a rearguard action by conservative historians at a time when a growing number of scholarly works indicated that the Nazi period could neither be confined to a so-called criminal clique nor traced back to foreign origins, nor indeed be presented as a reaction to even greater dangers. And yet, although the "revisionists" themselves have been largely discredited, the sensibilities they reflected have not gone away, indeed, have surfaced repeatedly since then in reaction to a new wave of works on the Nazi era and in the context of a newly unified Germany.

One such case has been the controversial and unique exhibition *The German Army and Genocide*. Circulating in Germany and Austria since 1995, and provoking a flood of media reports, political pronouncements and academic responses, the exhibition was the first public display of documents and photographs collected in German archives, and especially in the archives of the former Soviet Union and other East European states formerly under communist domination, concerning the criminal conduct of German soldiers in the East during World War II. What was most shocking to many German visitors and commentators was the clear evidence that the *Wehrmacht* was deeply involved not "only" in killing POWs and partisans or in carrying out large-scale operations of collective punishment against civilians, but also, in a direct and massive manner, in the implementation of the Final Solution. The exhibition unleashed a public debate over the extent to which the *Wehrmacht* could indeed be called a criminal organization, a designation that had previously been eschewed by most scholars ever since the Nuremberg Trials, where only the SS was seen as worthy of that title.[23]

Among the many reactions to the exhibition (which some cities in Germany refused to host and which met with especially strong opposition in Bavaria and Austria) was a series of articles in the influential weekly *Die Zeit*, subsequently published in a special issue under the title *Gerhorsam bis zum Mord? Der verschwiegene Krieg der deutschen Wehrmacht (Obedience to Murder? The Hidden War of the German Wehrmacht).*[24] Clearly, the argument of the exhibition touched a raw nerve, for here one could no longer speak of excesses by individuals or a few criminal generals, nor about SS atrocities or crimes committed "behind the back of the fighting troops," since the evidence was there for all to see: photographs taken by the soldiers themselves of massacres, hangings and torture, documents directing military units to murder Jewish communities, clear indications of the close collaboration between the SS and the regular army. Moreover, an important article by one of the organizers, Hannes Heer, presented previously unknown documents taken from newly opened archives, showing the process whereby *Wehrmacht* units had become directly involved in genocide.[25] Heer's findings were obviously only the tip of the iceberg and indicated that further research in formerly inaccessible archives would possibly lead to far more information on this dark episode in the *Wehrmacht's* history. Once more, the conventions of scholarship on the army's involvement in Nazi policies were shaken, and many old assumptions had to be revised.

Indeed, even before the storm over the exhibition had receded, Germany found itself embroiled in an even bigger and more disturbing controversy. The book that caused the row, Daniel Jonah Goldhagen's *Hitler's Willing Executioners: Ordinary Germans and the Holocaust*, is only marginally relevant to this article.[26] But the debate in Germany is highly revealing and tells us a great deal about the difficulties Germans still face in relating the Holocaust to actual flesh-and-blood killers rather than to anonymous forces or evil leaders.[27] For whatever the faults of the book in question (and they are many), it shows in no uncertain terms the involvement of middle-aged German men, not distinguished by either ideological fervor or political affiliation, in the

brutal torture and murder of thousands of Jews in face-to-face situations which, at least initially, they could have in fact chosen to avoid. If the book is written with a great deal of passion and rage (which does not add to its argument but has increased its appeal to readers), reactions in Germany were also passionate and often ill-considered. Although the killers with whom Goldhagen is concerned were not soldiers, they in many ways resembled the type of reservists one would have encountered in any number of regular army units. That they apparently not only willingly killed Jews but also enjoyed their "work" was highly unsettling to a public grown used to far more detached interpretations of that past and to explanatory models which kept the horror and gore at bay.

The storm over Goldhagen's book is thus related to the general reluctance to accept the involvement of regular army soldiers in the Holocaust. Since the men of the reserve police battalions greatly resembled the so-called "sober" army reservists who were said to have been mainly concerned with their own survival,[28] one could assume that the latter might just as readily have taken part in, and derived pleasure from, the mass murder of men, women, and children. This would in turn mean that millions of Germans who came back from the war in 1945 could have well been, at one time or another in their military career, "willing executioners." To be sure, this vision of a postwar Germany inhabited by innumerable killers contradicts Goldhagen's more comforting assertion that the Germans had miraculously been transformed after 1945 or 1949 and no longer harbored the anti-Semitic sentiments he believes were the main motivation for the Holocaust. But this is only one of the many contradictions in a work whose main importance and interest lies in its reception rather than in its inherent value as a scholarly study.[29]

Just as the storm over Goldhagen's book seems to be ebbing (though it is has now begun in France and Italy with the recent publication of the book in those countries),[30] another revelation promises to fuel the

debate over the *Wehrmacht* and further clarify the links between the case of the police battalions and the criminal activities of the regular soldiers. Recent reports inform us that some 1.3 million pages of cables sent by German murder squads in summer 1941, which were intercepted and decoded by British signals intelligence but have only now been declassified by the United States National Security Agency, clearly show that not only SS and police units but also regular army formations were involved in mass killings of Jews from the very first days of "Barbarossa," the German invasion of the Soviet Union launched on 22 June 1941. Although much of this has been known before, these documents provide more details on the beginning of the Holocaust and the apparently universal participation of German agencies on the ground in its implementation. Quite apart from raising questions about Allied reactions to mass killings, since contrary to their subsequent assertions of ignorance they now appear to have had the information right at their fingertips, these cables are certain to ignite another debate over the participation of the fighting troops—the professional soldiers—in genocide. Moreover, it has also been reported that the Russian government has handed some 15,000 documents of its own to the United States Holocaust Memorial Museum, which include information collected by Russian agents behind the lines, translations of German documents, and eyewitness accounts compiled by the Soviet War Crimes Commission at the end of the war.[31] All of this, along with an unknown number of documents still being unearthed in Russian and East European archives, is certain to significantly enhance our knowledge on this period and seems to point in the direction of far more killers and accomplices, and higher numbers of victims, than had been previously estimated, not least due to the direct involvement of the *Wehrmacht* in the killing. There may of course still be room to debate the question of whether the *Wehrmacht* as such was a criminal, indeed a genocidal, organization; but its participation in genocide on a grand scale seems no longer in doubt.

Notes

1. On formation chronicles and generals' memoirs, see Omer Bartov, *The Eastern Front, 1941-1945: German Troops and the Barbarization of Warfare* (London, 1985), 1-4, and the literature cited therein. On German film in the 1950s, see Heide Fehrenbach, *Cinema in Democratizing Germany: Reconstructing National Identity after Hitler* (Chapel Hill, NC, 1995). For examples of German magazine covers between 1950 and 1962 relating to this theme, see *Mittelweg 36* 5, no. 1 (1996): 1-9. On the debate over German rearmament and its implications for the image of the *Wehrmacht*, see David Clay Large, *Germans to the Front: West German Rearmament in the Adenauer Era* (Chapel Hill, NC, 1996); Donald Abenheim, *Reforging the Iron Cross: The Search for Tradition in the West German Armed Forces* (Princeton, 1988).

2. Hermann Graml et al., *The German Resistance to Hitler* (London, 1970). See also Peter Hoffmann, *The History of the German Resistance, 1933-1945* (Cambridge, MA, 1977); Joachim C. Fest, *Plotting Hitler's Death: The Story of the German Resistance* (New York, 1996); and Inge Scholl, *The White Rose: Munich, 1942-1943*, 2d ed. (Hanover, NH, 1983).

3. See, for example, B. H. Liddell Hart, *The Other Side of the Hill* (London, 1948); Desmond Young, *Rommell: The Desert Fox* (New York, 1950).

4. See, for example, James F. Tent, *Mission on the Rhine: Re-education and Denazification in American-Occupied Germany* (Chicago, 1982); C. Fitzgibbon, *Denazification* (London, 1969).

5. Large, *Germans to the Front.*

6. On the role of philo-Semitism in this process, see also Frank Stern, *The Whitewashing of the Yellow Badge: Antisemitism and Philosemitism in Postwar Germany* (Oxford, 1992).

7. Elazar Barkan is currently completing a book on the role of restitution in normalizing international relations and reducing the potential for conflict between governments and ethnic or cultural minorities. On the debate in Israel over the reparations agreement with Germany, see Tom Segev, *The Seventh Million: The Israelis and the Holocaust* (New York, 1993), 189-252.

8. See further in Omer Bartov, "The Missing Years: German Workers, German Soldiers," in David Crew, ed., *Nazism and German Society, 1933-1945* (London, 1944), 41-66.

9. Gerhard Ritter, *The German Problem: Basic Questions of German Political Life, Past and Present* (1948; Columbus, 1965); Friedrich Meinecke, *The German Catastrophe: Reflections and Recollections*, 2d ed. (1946; Boston, 1963); Heinz Guderian, *Panzer Leader*, 3d ed. (1952; London, 1977); Erich von Manstein, *Verlorene Siege*, 2d ed. (Frankfurt/Main, 1964); B. H. Liddell Hart, *History of the Second World War, 1939-45* (London, 1947); Gordon A. Craig, *The Politics of the Prussian Army, 1640-1945*, 3d ed. (1955; London, 1978); John Wheeler-Bennett, *The Nemesis of Power: The German Army in Politics, 1918-1945*, 2nd ed. (1953; London, 1980).

10. *Das Deutsche Reich und der Zweite Weltkrieg*, ed. Militärgeschichtliches Forschungsamt (Stuttgart, 1979-). Until now 6 volumes have been published but of at least 10, but more likely 12, planned.

11. Hans-Adolf Jacobsen, "Kommissarbefehi and Massenexekutionen sowjetsche Kriegsgefangener," in Hans Buchheim et al., eds., *Anatomie des SS-Staates* (Olten, 1965). This essay is not included in the abridged paperback English translation, Helmut Krausnick and Martin Broszat, *Anatomy of the SS State* (London, 1970).

12. Manfred Messerschmidt, *Die Wehrmacht im NS-Staat: Zeit der Indoktrination* (Hamburg, 1969); Christian Streit, *Keine Kameraden: Die Wehrmacht und die sowjetischen Kriegsgefangenen, 1941-1945* (Stuttgart, 1978); see also Alfred Streim, *Die Behandlung sowjetischer Kriegsgefangener im "Fall Barbarossa."* Ein Dokumentation (Heidelberg, 1981); Helmut Krausnick and Hans-Heinrich Wilhelm, *Die Truppe des Weltanschauungskrieges: Die Einsatzgruppen der Sicher-heitspolizei und des SD, 1938-1942* (Stuttgart, 1981).

13. Volker R. Berghahn, "NSDAP und 'Geistige Führung' der Wehrmacht," *Vierteljahrshefte für Zeitgeschichte* (hereafter *VfZ*) 17 (1969): 17-21; Klaus-Jürgen Müller, *Das Heer und Hitler: Armee und nationalsozialistisches Regime, 1933-1940* (Stuttgart, 1969).

14. Horst Boog et al., *Der Angriff auf die Sowjetunion* (Stuttgart, 1983), vol. 4 of *Das Deutsche Reich und der Zweite Weltkrieg*.

15. Alexander Dallin, *German Rule in Russia 1941-45: A Study of Occupation Policies* (London, 1957); Robert J. O'Neill, *The German Army and the Nazi Party, 1933-39* (London, 1966).

16. See, for example, Martin Broszat and Elke Fröhlich, *Alltag und Widerstand: Bayern im Nationalsozialismus* (Munich, 1987). At the back of this volume is a list of all the studies published in 6 volumes in 1977-1983 in the series edited by Broszat, *Bayern in der NS-Zeit*. See also Klaus Bergmann and Rolf Schörcken, eds., *Geschichte im Alltag—Alltag in der Geschichte* (Düsseldorf, 1982); Harald Focke and Monika Stroka, *Alltag der Gleichgeschalteten: Wie die Nazis Kirche, Kultur, Justiz und Presse braun färbten* (Reinbeck bei Hamburg, 1985), vol. 3 of Rowohlt Verlag's series *Alltag unterm Hakenkreuz*; Ian Kershaw, *Popular Opinion and Political Dissent in the Third Reich: Bavaria 1933-1945* (Oxford, 1983), a much expanded version of an essay originally published in Broszat's above-mentioned series. More generally on Alltags-geschichte, see Alf Lüdtke, ed., *The History of Everyday Life: Reconstructing Historical Experience and Ways of Life* (Princeton, 1965).

17. See, for example, William Sheridan Allan, *The Nazi Seizure of Power: The Experience of a Single German Town, 1930-1935* (New York, 1965); Rudy Koshar, "Two Nazisms': The Social Context, of Nazi Mobilization in Marburg and Tübingen," *Social History 7* (1982); Herbert Schwarzwälder, *Die Machter-greifung der NSDAP in Bremen 1933* (Bremen, 1966).

18. Apart from the literature cited above, see also the comments in Hans Mommsen, "Kriegserfahrungen," in Ulrich Borsdorf and Mathilde Jamin, eds., *Uber Leben im Krieg: Kriegserfahrungen in eine Industrieregion, 1939-1945* (Reinbeck bei Hamburg, 1989), esp. 13.

19. Bartov, *Eastern Front*; idem, *Hitler's Army: Soldiers, Nazis, and War in the Third Reich* (New York, 1991); Theo Schulte, *The German Army and Nazi Polices in Occupied Russia* (Oxford, 1989); Stephen Fritz, *Frontsoldaten: The German Soldier in World War II* (Kentucky, 1995); Thomas Kühne, "Kameradschaft—'Das Beste im Leben des Mannes': Die deutsche Soldaten des II. Weltkrieges in erfahrungs- und geschlechtergeschichtlicher perspektive" (unpublished manuscript); idem, "'... aus diesem Krieg werden nicht nur harte Männer heimkehren': Kriegskameradschaft und Männlichkeit im 20. Jahrhundert," in idem, ed., *Männergeschichte—Geschlechtergeschichte: Männlichkeit im Wandel der Moderne* (Frankfurt/Main, 1996). More generally, recent important work in this genre includes Stéphane Audoin-Rouzeau, *Men at War, 1914-1918: National Sentiment and Trench Journalism in France during the First World War* (Providence, 1992); Leonard V. Smith, *Between Mutiny and Obedience: The Case of the French Fifth Infantry Division during World War I* (Princeton, 1994); Gerhard Hirschfeld et al., eds., *Keiner fühlt sich hier mehr als Mensch... Erlebnis und Wirkung des Ersten Weltkriegs* (Essen, 1993); Detlev Vogel and Wofram Wette, eds., *Andere Helme—Andere Menschen? Heimaterfahrung und Frontalltag im Zweiten Weltkrieg. Ein Internationaler Vergleich* (Essen, 1995).

20. Most of the important contributions to the debate are now available in *Forever in the Shadow of Hitler? Original Documents of the Historikerstreit, the Controversy Concerning the Singularity of the Holocaust*, ed. and trans. James Knowlton and Truett Cates (Atlantic Highlands, NJ, 1993).

21. Andreas Hillgruber, *Zweierlei Untergang: Die Zerschlagung des deutschen Reiches und das Ende des europäischen Judentums* (Berlin, 1986). See also Omer Bartov, "Historians on the Eastern Front: Andreas Hillgruber and Germany's Tragedy," in idem, *Murder in Our Midst: The Holocaust, Industrial Killing, and Representation* (New York, 1996), 71-88.

22. Richard Evans, *In Hitler's Shadow: West German Historians and the Attempt to Escape from the Nazi Past* (New York, 1989); Hans-Ulrich Wehler, *Entr-sorgung der deutschlen Vergangenheit? Ein polemischer Essay zum "Historikerstreit"* (Munich, 1988); Charles S. Maier, *The Unmasterable Past: History, Holocaust, and German National Identity* (Cambridge, MA, 1988).

23. For a report on the exhibition, relevant publications and media reactions to it in Germany, see Klaus Naumann, "Wenn ein Tabu bricht: Die Wehrmachts-Ausstellung in der Bundesrepublik"; and in Austria, Walter Manoschek, "Die Wehrmacht-sausstellung in Österreich: Ein Bericht," both in

*Mittelweg 36* 5, no. 1 (1996): 11-24 and 25-32, respectively. The essay collection is Hannes Heer and Klaus Naumann, eds., *Vernichtungskrieg: Verbrechen der Wehrmacht, 1941-1944* (Hamburg, 1995).

24. *Zeit-Punkte: Gerhorsam bis zum Mord? Der verschwiegene Krieg der deutschen Wehrmacht— Fakten, Analysen, Debatte* (Hamburg, n.d.).

25. Hannes Heer, "Killing Fields: Die Wehrmacht und der Holocaust," in *Vernichtungskrieg*, 57-77.

26. Daniel Jonah Goldhagen, *Hitler's Willing Executioners: Ordinary Germans and the Holocaust* (New York, 1996). For a critique of the book, see Omer Bartov, "Ordinary Monsters," *New Republic*, 29 Apr. 1996, 32-38; Christopher R. Browning, "Daniel Goldhagen's Willing Executioners," *History & Memory* 8, no. 1 (Spring/Summer 1996): 88-108.

27. Many of the contributions to the debate have now been published in Julius Schoeps, ed., *Ein Volk von Mördern? Die Dokumentation zur Goldhagen-Kontroverse umd ie Rolle der Deutschen im Holocaust* (Hamburg, 1996).

28. Mommsen, "Kriegserfahrungen." Note, for example, the concluding remarks in the introduction to the chronicle of the 18th Panzer Division, whose involvement in the implementation of Nazi policies and the ideological indoctrination of its soldiers were documented in my book *The Eastern Front*. The author and former officer of that division writes: "None of those who did not return home wanted to go to that land [the USSR]; none of them wanted to occupy it. The records of the 18th Panzer Division ... are free of any ideological propaganda on our side. They are records of soldiers." Wolfgang Paul, *Geschichte der 18. Panzer-Division, 1940-1943* (Freiburg, n.d.).

29. The debate over the *Wehrmachtsausstellung* has recently been revived following the arrival of the exhibition in Munich. See Theo Sommer, "Münchner Lektionen: Die Rolle der Wehrmacht läßt sich nicht beschönigen," *Die Zeit*, 28 Feb. 1997; Rudolf Augstein, "Anschlag auf die 'Ehre' des deutschen Soldaten?" *Der Spiegel*, no. 11 (1997); Alan Cowell, "The Past Erupts in Munich as War Guilt Is Put on Display," *New York Times*, 3 Mar. 1997. See further Ruth Beckermann's recent documentary film, *Jenseits des Krieges*, on the reception of the Wehrmacht exhibition in Vienna.

30. See, for example, Édouard Husson, "Le phénomène Goldhagen," and Philippe Burrin, "Il n'y a pas de peuple assassin!" both in *L'histoire* 206 (Jan. 1997): 80-85.

31. David Hoffman, "U.S. Holocaust Museum Gets KGB Files," *Washington Post Foreign Service*, 29 Oct. 1996, A12; Michael Dobbs, "Decoded Cables Revise History of Holocaust: German Police Implicated; British Knew," *Washington Post*, 10 Nov. 1996, A1; Bronwen Maddox, "British Knew Jews Were Being Killed 'before Auschwitz'," *Times*, 11 Nov. 1996; Alan Cowel, "Files Suggest British Knew Early of Nazi Atrocities Against Jews," *New York Times*, 19 Nov. 1996, A1, A6; transcript (from WWW) of interview on the PBS television "Newshour with Jim Lehrer," "What the Allies Knew: Charles Krause Speaks with Richard Breitman," 20 Nov. 1996.

Bernd Boll and Hannes Heer  Prologue

The International Military Tribunal in Nuremberg commenced proceedings against governmental, party and military leaders of the Nazi state at the end of 1945, accusing them of crimes against peace, war crimes, and crimes against humanity.

Of the five military leaders charged, three were sentenced to death, one was sentenced to life in prison, and one to twenty years imprisonment. The court refrained from declaring the High Command of the *Wehrmacht* a "criminal organization" for formal reasons since it did not fulfill its definition of an organization.

Nonetheless, after assessing the existing evidence, the judges left no doubt that the *Wehrmacht* was involved in *"crimes on a scale larger and more shocking than the world has ever had the misfortune to know."* The judges called upon the authorities to bring every individual suspected of having committed crimes before a court. As a result, hundreds of officers of the German *Wehrmacht* were sentenced to severe punishment.

Despite this unambiguous declaration by the international community, the *Wehrmacht* generals continued to circulate a legend they had propagated immediately after their defeat in 1945: The legend of the "unsullied *Wehrmacht*."

According to this legend, the *Wehrmacht* kept its distance from Hitler and the National Socialist regime, fulfilled its soldierly duty with decency and dignity and was informed about the atrocities committed by Hitler's *Sonderkommandos* only after the fact, if at all.

Now, more than fifty years later, it is time to renounce this lie once and for all and to accept the reality of a huge crime:

From 1939 through 1944, the *Wehrmacht* did not wage a "normal, decent war", but rather, a war of annihilation against prisoners of war, Jews, and other civilians, a war with millions of victims.

The exhibition presents three exemplary cases: Serbia, White Russia, and the Ukraine. Furthermore, it depicts how the National Socialist war of annihilation was prepared from 1933 on, and rehearsed for the first time in Poland in 1939. The intention of the exhibition is not only to promote debate on the *Wehrmacht's* involvement in genocide, but also to contribute to discussion on the barbarity of war in modern times.

Bernd Boll, Hannes Heer, and Walter Manoschek

## Prelude to a Crime: The German Army in the National Socialist State, 1933–1939

Hitler, as the leader of the National Socialist German Workers' Party, which had won the largest number of seats in the *Reichstag* in the November 1932 elections, was named Reich Chancellor on January 30, 1933. Hitler's government found its most faithful allies among the conservative elites and in the Army.

Following the introduction of compulsory military service in 1935, the *Wehrmacht* quickly grew to 36 divisions with a total of 550,000 soldiers. The traditional "Prussian" army generals identified with Hitler's major goals.

The heavy influx of young recruits and reserve officers ensured that when the war began in 1939, the majority of enlisted men and officers of the *Wehrmacht* were men who had received a National Socialist education at school and in the numerous party organizations.

By the time the war began, the *Wehrmacht* had been transformed from an elite military caste into a "people's army." The *Wehrmacht* had become the *"second column" of the National Socialist State* (Hitler).

Wehrmacht and National Socialism: in part, identical goals

The generals welcomed the pronouncedly nationalist stance of the NSDAP and Hitler's intent to revise the 1919 Treaty of Versailles which limited the strength of the German Army to 100,000 men.

February 3, 1933:
Hitler promises the generals compulsory military service and proclaims the goal of acquiring "*Lebensraum* in the East and the ruthless Germanization of the area."

March 16, 1935:
Reintroduction of compulsory military service. The Western powers tolerate this breach of the Treaty of Versailles.

March 1936:
The *Wehrmacht* marches into the demilitarized Rhineland.

The *Wehrmacht*: the second column of the National Socialist state

In several speeches held soon after taking office as the Reich President, Hitler emphasized the role of *Wehrmacht* as the "second column" of the National Socialist state (with the Nazi Party as the first).

February 10, 1934
The national eagle with the swastika — the symbol of the NSDAP — becomes standard insignia on *Wehrmacht* uniforms.

May 25, 1934:
The duties of the German soldier are newly defined:

*The* Wehrmacht *is the arms bearer of the German people. It protects the German Reich and Fatherland, the people united in National Socialism, and its Leben-sraum. The roots of its strength lie in a glorious past, in the German* Volkstum, *and in the German soil and labor. Service in the* Wehrmacht *is a service of honor for the German people.*" (Heeres-Verordnungsblatt 1935)

June 30, 1934:
The German Armed Forces and the *Schutzstaffel* (SS) join in a common operation to eliminate the arms-bearing *Sturmabteilungen* (SA) of the NSDAP by force. Two army generals, von Schleicher and von Bredow, are murdered by the SS in the process; the army does not protest.

August 2, 1934:
Hitler becomes the Reich President and thus Commander-in-Chief of the *Wehrmacht*. As proof of loyalty and thanks for the elimination of the SA, Brigadier General Walter von Reichenau, the future head of the Sixth Army, formulates a *Wehrmacht* oath of personal allegiance to Hitler:
*"I swear this sacred oath by God that I will render absolute obedience to the* Führer *of the German Reich and people, Adolf Hitler, the Commander-in Chief of the* Wehrmacht, *and will be prepared as a courageous soldier to offer my life at any time for this oath."*

A "Jew-free" *Wehrmacht*

Even before the Nuremberg race laws were established in September 1935, the *Wehrmacht* instituted the first anti-Semitic measures among its own ranks.

February 2, 1934:
Discharge of all Jewish officers and soldiers from the *Wehrmacht*.

December 21, 1934:
Officers may not marry Jews.

September 15, 1935:
Jews were prohibited from active military service; so-called "Jewish *Mischlinge* (those of mixed Jewish and "Aryan" descent) were not allowed to occupy positions of authority:

*"Aryan descent is a prerequisite for active military service. Only Aryans can engage in active duty and occupy positions of authority. Active duty and reserve* Wehrmacht *personnel of Aryan descent are forbidden to enter into marriages with persons of non-Aryan descent."* (Wehrgesetz, June 1936)

The *Wehrmacht* included anti-Semitic texts in its instructional material:
*"We Germans are presently fighting a double battle. With respect to all non-Jewish peoples, we merely wish to assert our vital interests. We respect them and are engaged in a chivalrous conflict with them. We are fighting world Jewry, however, as one would fight a noxious parasite; it is not only an enemy of our people, but a plague on all peoples. The battle against the Jews is a moral battle for the purity and health of the divinely created* Volksstum *and for a new, more just order in the world."*
(Der Jude in der Deutschen Geschichte, in: Schulung-shefte für den Unterricht über nationalsozialistische Weltanschauung und nationalpolitische Zielsetzung, ed. by the High Command of the *Wehrmacht*, vol. 5, 1939)

First annexations

February 4, 1938:
Hitler dismisses the War Minister and Commander-in-Chief of the *Wehrmacht*, Werner von Blomberg, and the Commander-in-Chief of the *Wehrmacht*, Freiherr von Fritsch, and himself assumes supreme command over the military forces.

March 13, 1938:
Austria is invaded by the *Wehrmacht* and annexed by Germany.

September 29, 1938:
Munich Pact: Annexation of the Sudeten region by Germany.

March 16, 1939:
Occupation of the remaining parts of Czechoslovakia; Slovakia constitutes itself as a puppet state of the Third Reich.

1939/40:
The assault on Poland: genocide begins

Hitler's charge to the *Wehrmacht*

After the First World War, one of the declared aims of German foreign policy was to reclaim territory lost to Poland in 1919. After taking power in 1933, the National Socialists began to expand this goal into a racially determined politics of "*Lebensraum.*"

The non-aggression pact with Stalin signed on August 23, 1939 provided Hitler with the political prerequisites for the invasion of Poland. This temporary alliance of convenience with Stalin provided for the division of Poland between Germany and the Soviet Union; for Hitler, it warded off the danger of a war on two fronts. On the very day agreement was reached on the treaty, Hitler sketched his expectations for the course of the war in Poland for an audience of *Wehrmacht* generals:

*"Politically there had been a remarkable achievement, now the* Wehrmacht *would have to prove itself and demonstrate its ability. The war would be waged with the greatest brutality and ruthlessness and until Poland was totally destroyed. The goal was not to occupy land but to annihilate all forces. He would create the reason for the war. Later in history no one would ask about the reasons."* (Hitler's speech at the Berghof on August 22, 1939, according to the diary of Helmuth Greiner.)

Hitler's charge included not only military aims, but also other measures motivated by racist ideology. In order to secure *Lebensraum* in Eastern Europe,

• Western Poland was to be "cleansed" of Poles and Jews, incorporated into the German Reich, and settled by ethnic Germans.

• The Polish elite (nobility, priests, intellectuals) were to be exterminated and the Poles considered "racially useful" were to be "Germanized."

• The remaining Poles were to serve the German "master race" as uneducated slaves in Eastern Poland.

• The Jewish population was to be decimated and driven into Eastern Poland.

## Reactions of the generals

The *Einsatzgruppen* of the Security Police and of the Security Service (SD) were responsible for carrying out the racist program to "Germanize" Poland. They received their orders to kill from Heinrich Himmler, but were dependent on the *Wehrmacht* for fuel, ammunition, and provisions.

While individual commanders of the Army such as General Blaskowitz criticized this cooperation with the *Einsatzgruppen*, others, like General von Brauchitsch or General von Küchler, expressed their understanding of these politically and ideologically motivated mass murders.

General Johannes Blaskowitz: Commander-in-Chief East:

*"Communication with organs of the Security Police and Order Police has been quite troubled since the Governor General took over the civilian administration. Furthermore the troops do not want to be identified with the atrocities committed by the Security Police, and refuse any cooperation with these Einsatzgruppen, which serve almost exclusively as execution squads. Up to now the police have not functioned in any visible way to create order, but have only spread terror among the population."*
(The Commander-in-Chief East, Johannes Blakowitz, to the Commander-in-Chief of the Army, Walther von Brauchitsch, November 27, 1939)

General Walter von Brauchitsch, Commander-in-Chief of the Army:

*"The execution of tasks dictated by our racial politics [Volkspolitische Aufgaben] which are essential for securing German Lebensraum and which the Führer has ordered carried out has already of necessity led to otherwise unusual and harsh measures against the Polish population in the occupied territory. The accelerated realization of these tasks, in preparation for the coming decisive struggle of the German people, has been accompanied, naturally enough, by a further intensification of such measures."*
(The Commander-in-Chief of the Army, Walther von Brauchitsch, to all army groups and armies, February 7, 1940)

Georg von Küchler, Commanding General XVIIIth Army Corps:

*"... I emphasize the necessity to see to it that all soldiers of the army, especially officers, refrain from any and all criticism of the battle with the population in the GG [General Government], for example, the treatment of Polish minorities, of Jews, and of church affairs. The völkische Final Solution of the struggle between peoples [Volkskampf] that has raged on the Eastern border for centuries requires especially harsh measures. Certain units of the party and of the state are entrusted with carrying out this völkische struggle in the East. Soldiers are to keep their distance from these affairs of other units. That means they are also not to criticize such undertakings ..."*
(Order of the Commanding General of the XVIIIth Army Corps, Georg von Küchler, July 22, 1940)

1–3: Shooting of 300 Polish civilians by soldiers of an infantry regiment, Ciepielów, September 1939 (see report below)

2

3

4: Photo by a German soldier with the notation: "A Pole came to meet the advancing troops: 'The city is peaceful!' Upon entering the town, our troops were fired on. . . ."

5: Unidentified locality, probably Lódz.

6: From the photo album of a soldier named Rothenberger. Handwritten note: "Jewess who was shot."

Crimes against prisoners of war and civilians

In Poland, from the beginning, the racist aims of the National Socialist leadership went hand in hand with the anti-Polish and anti-Semitic attitudes of soldiers of the *Wehrmacht*.

• Polish prisoners of war were often killed to the last man: 222 of them, for example, in Cwiklice, 200 in Zambrowo, and many hundreds in dozens of other cases.

The *Wehrmacht's* treatment of civilians who defended their towns against German troops was especially brutal. Orders required that they be shot immediately: 300 in Kleck, 200 in Zloczew, and hundreds more in many other locations.

• Acts of violence by the troops were also directed at unarmed civilians. Only a few days after the assault on Poland began, plundering and rapes reached such levels that the military leadership was repeatedly forced to take counter-measures.

The *Wehrmacht*, the police, *Einsatzgruppen* and the local ethnic German militias perpetrated killing actions as individual organizations, as well as together with others. Under the pretense of retaliation for sabotage, anti-German activity, armed insurgency, or simply because the victims were members of the Polish intelligentsia, these organizations committed massacres of Polish civilians each and every day in September and October 1939 — a total of 764 executions with approximately 20,000 victims. The *Wehrmacht* was responsible for 311 of these mass murders.

*"And now in the Ciepielów forest not far from Zwolén, the 11th company of our battalion was leading the advance. We follow them. I hear machine gun fire. Those in front have been shot at. Dismount . . . Ricochets are humming. I now realize that the Poles are also shooting . . . Captain von Lewinsky is the first to go spinning. Shot in the head from above. So, snipers in the trees. I admire the courage of these snipers in the trees . . . An hour later everyone gathers on the road. The company counts 14 dead, including Captain von Lewinsky. The regiment commander Colonel Wessel (from Kassel), with his monocle in his eye, was furious: 'What nerve, to think they could stop us and they shot my Lewinsky.' . . .*

*He asserts that these snipers were partisans, even though every one of the 300 Poles taken prisoner is wearing a uniform. They are forced to take off their jackets. There, now they look more like partisans. Now their suspenders are cut off, too, ostensibly so they can't run away. Now the prisoners have to walk along the edge of the road in single file. Where were they being lead, that was the question. Back to the rear, then to be taken to the next prisoner collecting point? Five minutes later, I hear 1 [one]dozen German machine pistols clattering. I hurry in that direction and I see, 100 meters to the rear, 300 Polish prisoners lying shot in the ditch running along the side of the road. I risk taking two photographs, then one of the armed motorcyclists who did the job on orders from Lieutenant Colonel Wessel posed proudly in front of my lens."*
(Report by a soldier of a motorized infantry regiment, September 1939)

*"Leokadia Podgorska, born on July 8, 1923, explains that she was forced by two soldiers to go into the bedroom of her parents. There the soldiers threw her onto one of the beds and in spite of defending herself and screaming with all her strength, they forced her to have sexual intercourse with them. While one soldier held her and pressed her into the pillows, the other soldier used her."*
(Report, September 16, 1939, Army Group Command South/Secret Field Police Group 520)

*"Sharp rise in plundering in Lódź by* Wehrmacht *personnel and civilians wearing armbands with swastikas."*
(Report by the Secret Field Police Group 540, September 23-30, 1939)

## The *Wehrmacht* and the Jews

The *Wehrmacht* took part in many acts of violence against Jews on its own initiative: humiliations, plundering, forced labor, expulsions. More than 20,000 Jews, including almost the entire Jewish population of Jaroslaw (Gestapo operation) and 4,000 from Tarnobrzeg (*Wehrmacht* operation), were driven out of the area north and east of Rzeszów at the end of September and beginning of October 1939.

The police and the *Einsatzgruppen* were primarily responsible for the murder of Jews. But *Wehrmacht* soldiers also took part. In September 1939 alone, they shot more than 1,200 Jews. Through the end of 1939, German occupation authorities assisted by the *Wehrmacht* murdered approximately 7,000 Polish Jews.

*"On Saturday, October 7, 1939, while walking through the town, I learned from conversations among comrades that a large number of Poles had been shot that morning at the Jewish cemetery in Sch[wetz] and that on Sunday morning a further shooting was to take place....*

*"I therefore went with most of my fellow-soldiers to the Jewish cemetery on Sunday morning ...*

*"We watched as a group consisting of a woman and three children, the children from about three to eight years of age, were led from a bus to a dug-out grave about 8 meters wide and 8 meters long. The woman was forced to climb down into this grave and carried her youngest child with her. The two other children were handed to her by two men of the execution squad. The woman had to lay down flat on her stomach, with her face to the earth, her three children lined up in the same way to her left.*

*"Then four men stepped into the grave, placed the muzzles of their rifles about 30 cm from the backs of the necks, and shot the woman with her three children. I was then told by the* Sturmbannführer *in charge to assist in shoveling dirt over the corpses. I obeyed the order and thus could observe from close up how the next groups of women and children were executed in a similar fashion. A total of 9-10 groups of women and children, each time four of them in the same mass grave.*

*"About 200* Wehrmacht *soldiers watched the shootings from a distance of about 30 meters. A little later a second bus drove up to the cemetery, carrying men with one woman among them.... A total of about 28 women, 25 men, and 10 children from 3-8 years old were executed on this morning."*
(Record of the interrogation of Private P. Kluge, Army Ambulance Section 581, about the SS massacre in Swiecie. On November 10, 1939, as quoted in the diary of Helmuth Groscurth, p. 406f.)

*"Today there was a surprise. I was at a Jew's to confiscate a radio (which, logically, he didn't have). When I drew my pistol, however, and told him to move back three steps, he came up with the radio, and to our surprise he had 130 bottles of wine and seven kegs of 250 liters. We opened several bottles and made him drink first so we were certain, whether [sic] the wine was not poisoned. If he drinks, we can drink too. Okay, woman, cheers! With us, it is - we are in enemy territory and I trust no one: I'd rather let my pistol speak than be the one to go, for we've got plenty of ammunition. For if you see those kinds of people, you can scarcely fathom that it's still possible in the 20th Century. The Jews want to kiss our hand but we draw our pistols and hear `God help us' and he [sic] runs away as fast as he can."*
(Letter from the field, Franz P., 1st Company, 521st Guard Battalion, to his wife, September 21, 1939)

*"On September 11, traveled on via Tarnów in the night to Jaroslaw. Here there were an awful lot of Jews, the usual Eastern Jews with beards. The SS organized whole companies of Jews to clean and clear things up. They had to supply the implements and, of course, work for nothing ...*

*"Understandably, our supplies are sometimes late and in that case we requisition what we need, first in Jewish shops, recently we got twelve eggs per man for one day."*
(Letter from the field, Richard T. v. F., 2nd Company of the 70th Engineer Battalion, September 17, 1939)

*"Near Pultusk the troops shot 80 Jews down like animals."*
(From the diary of Colonel Helmuth Groscurth, head of the Unit for Special Duty, Army General Staff, September 22, 1939)

The Massacre in Konskie, September 12, 1939

Four German soldiers had died in skirmishes in the course of a few days. The *Wehrmacht* dragged about 40 Jews from nearby homes, among them many old men (1–2), to dig graves for the soldiers' burial in the market place (5). German soldiers who were watching spread the rumor that the dead had been mutilated by Polish civilians. The Jews dug a pit (3–4) which they thought was to be their own grave and were brutally beaten by *Wehrmacht* soldiers in the process. But after the work was done, the Jews were chased away and ran panic-stricken across the market place. Soldiers fired at them and a bloodbath commenced. In the end, 19 Jews lay dead on the street, 3 others died in the next few days (10–11). A prominent German film director was one of the onlookers: Leni Riefenstahl, who had volunteered to go to the front as a reporter (6–9).

1

2

3

4

5

6

7

8

9

10

11

1940/41
Preparation for the war against the Soviet Union

Hitler's goal: racial war in the East

In his programmatic book Mein Kampf, written in 1924/25, Hitler declared that a new war was unavoidable. The opponent in this battle was to be the Jewish people, a "cancerous growth" on history, and — as "the most horrible example" of Jewish hegemony — Bolshevism.

The goal of this future armed conflict was the extermination of the Jewish-Bolshevist "blight on the world" and the acquisition of *Lebensraum* in the East. Because the existence of the German people supposedly depended on the realization of this goal, the war in the East was a "just war" and could be waged by even "the most inhuman means." After assuming power on January 30, 1933, Hitler began to prepare for this war with massive rearmament, the reintroduction of compulsory military service, and racist indoctrination of the *Wehrmacht*. After the "Anti-Comintern Pact," which was directed against Moscow, was signed in November 1936, the Nazis began a propaganda offensive against "Jewish-Bolshevism" and the "Russian Untermensch." An exhibition visited by millions of Germans promised to show "Bolshevism unmasked."

In speeches held in the Reichstag in 1937 and 1938, Hitler called upon the Germans to fight against *"Jewish international Bolshevism from Moscow."*

On January 30, 1939, he prophesied in the Reichstag that if the Jewish people succeeded in plunging Germany into a war, the result would not be "the Bolshevization of the world and thus the victory of the Jews, but the annihilation of the Jewish race in Europe." A week later he detailed this prophecy for his generals: the next war would be "a pure war of *Weltanschauung,* that is a deliberate war between peoples [Volkskrieg] and race war."

Poster for the exhibition "Bolshevism Unmasked," which opened November 1937 in the Reichstag Building in Berlin and shown in German cities until August 1939.

*"It is the most shameful exhibition I have ever seen. . . . The pictures show Communist atrocities in all countries of the world, and the Communists are all Jews. There are depictions of murders, rapes, thefts, revolutions, and armed uprisings. There is no imaginable crime of which Jews and Communists are not guilty."*
(Diary entry of the U. S. Ambassador in Berlin, William E. Dodd, December 26, 1937)

Criminal orders

The meticulously disguised preparations for the attack on the Soviet Union, the so-called "Operation Barbarossa" began in July 1940 after the victory over France.

Plans for the war were based on Hitler's programmatic instructions for a "*Volkskrieg* and race war": the political elite and the Jewish population were to be annihilated, the remaining population was to be decimated by a further 20 to 30 million and those left alive were to be employed as slaves in the service of German settlers.

Such a war could only be waged by disregarding internationally recognized conventions of war and international law. The four key orders of the campaign were based on that assumption and openly and unabashedly called upon soldiers to engage in criminal actions:

• Soviet prisoners of war were not to be viewed as defeated "fellow-soldiers" but rather as politically indoctrinated criminals of "treacherous" character who thus had

*"lost every right to treatment . . . according to the Geneva Convention."*
(Orders of June 16, 1941 and September 8, 1941)

• The civilian population deserved special treatment. Instead of bringing civilians before a military court as provided by international law,

*"the troops [were permitted] to defend themselves ruthlessly against every threat by the hostile civilian population."*
There was to be no punishment for criminal acts committed by individual German soldiers against the civilian population unless such acts undermined the discipline of the troops.
(Order of May 13, 1941)

• Political commissars were seen as the actual "perpetrators of resistance" and *"the originators of barbaric Asiatic fighting methods"*. In dealings with them, any *"regard for international law"* was uncalled for. They were to be *"finished off with weapons immediately as a matter of principle."*
(Order of June 6, 1941)

*"Our tasks in Russia: destroy the armed forces, dissolve the state . . .*
*"The battle of two Weltanschauungen against one another. A scathing appraisal of Bolshevism, is equivalent to asocial criminality. Communism a horrible danger for the future.*
*"We must distance ourselves from the standpoint of soldierly comradery. The Communist was not a fellow-soldier before captivity and will not be afterward. This is a battle of annihilation. . . .*
*"The battle must be waged against the poison of subversion. This is not a matter for martial law. The leaders of the troops must know what we are dealing with. They must be leaders in the battle.*
*"The troops must defend themselves with the same means that are being used against them.*
*"Commissars and GPU people [Soviet secret police in the 1930s] are criminals and must be treated as such....*
*"This struggle will be very different from the battle in the West. In the East, harshness is gentleness for the future.*
*"The leaders must themselves make the sacrifice of overcoming their doubts."*
(Hitler's remarks to the Generals on March 30, 1941; notes by Chief of the General Staff of the Army, Franz Halder)

*"The war against Russia is an essential stage in the existential battle of the German people. It is the ancient battle of the Germanic peoples against the Slavs, the defense of European culture against Muscovite-Asiatic floods, the repulsion of Jewish-Bolshevism. "This struggle must have as its goal the destruction of contemporary Russia and thus must be conducted with unheard of harshness...*
(Order of the Commander of the 4th Panzer Group, General Hoepner, on future warfare in the East, May 2, 1941)

*"1. Bolshevism is the deadly enemy of the National Socialist German people. This subversive Weltanschauung and its advocates are the targets of Germany's struggle.*

*"2. This struggle calls for ruthless and energetic action against Bolshevist agitators, irregulars, saboteurs, Jews, and the total suppression of every active or passive resistance.*

*"5. . . . The USSR is a political structure that unites a large number of Slavic, Caucasian, and Asiatic peoples and that is held together by the force of the Bolshevik ruling powers. Jews are heavily represented in the USSR.*
(Rules for the Conduct of Troops in Russia, May 19, 1941)

• Jews were to be eliminated. An agreement between the *Wehrmacht* and the SS clarified the arrangements for murder: *Einsatzgruppen* of the SS were assigned to cooperate with frontline troops as well as Army units in the rear. The *Einsatzgruppen* were to complete *"their tasks on their own responsibility"* and were placed under *Wehrmacht* command *"with respect to marches, provisions, and shelter."*
The leaders of the SS were required to *"report in a timely manner"* their murders to *Wehrmacht* commanders and to cultivate a *"continuous close collaboration"* with the responsible staff officers.
(Order of April 28, 1941)

Ulrich von Hassell
(1881-1944)
Ambassador in Rome 1932-1938

Von Hassell worked actively for the overthrow of the Hitler government and was executed in Berlin-Plötzensee following the July 20, 1944 attempt to assassinate Hitler.

*May 4, 1941*
*"On April 8 I was with Hase [Oster] and D[ohnanyi] at Geibel's [Beck] and the documented information we received there made one's hair stand on end: orders issued to the troops, signed by Halder, about how to proceed in Russia and about the systematic transformation of military justice, as applied to the population, into an uncontrolled caricature, which makes a parody of any law . . .*
*"With this submission to Hitler's orders, Br[auchitsch] sacrifices the honor of the German Army."*

*June 15, 1941*
*"Repeated long discussions with Geißler [Popitz], Pfaff [Goerdeler] and Hase [Oster] and others, among other things about the question of whether the orders just received but not yet passed on by the leaders of the Army, orders concerning brutal, uncontrolled actions of the troops against the Bolsheviks during the march into Russia, are not at last sufficient to open the eyes of the military leadership to the spirit of the regime for which they are fighting. We reached the conclusion that, once again, one could expect nothing. Brauchitsch and Halder have already given in to Hitler's maneuver to transfer the odium of murder and incendiarism from the SS, which is to date solely tainted, to the Army . . .*
*"Hopeless sergeants!"*
(Entries in the diary of Ulrich von Hassel, May 4, 1941 and June 15, 1941, using false names)

Was there resistance?

Highly qualified military officers with long service in rank were responsible for all of these murderous orders: In the High Command of the *Wehrmacht* (OKW) by Keitel, Chief of the *Wehrmacht* High Command and his associates Jodl and Warlimont, in the High Command of the Army (OKH) by Commander-in-Chief von Brauchitsch and his Chief of Staff Halder. The commanders of the *Luftwaffe* and Navy were involved in the planning, all commanders who later participated in the war in the East were informed.

None of these high-ranking officers protested against the *Wehrmacht*'s cooperation with the *Einsatzkommandos* in murdering Jews, because, as Field Marshal Keitel explained before the Nuremberg Tribunal, it was "*well-known*" that "*the officer corps in general viewed the Jews with distaste.*"

Several military leaders, such as the Commander of the Army Group Center von Bock, criticized the troops' license for absolute terror among the civilian population. Admiral Canaris, head of the Intelligence office, pointed out that the treatment of prisoners of war violated international law. After their protests brought no change, both of them made sure that the orders they had criticized were carried out. As a result of these orders, thousands of commissars, more than three million prisoners of war, approximately two million Jews, and more than five million other civilians were murdered from 1941 through 1944.

Only after the war had gone on for some time did an organized form of resistance develop among officers, in the face of the genocide being practiced daily and the threat of military defeat. This resistance culminated in the failed attempt to assassinate Hitler by Count Klaus von Stauffenberg on July 20, 1944. In May/June 1941, before the attack on the Soviet Union, only a few people, most of them civilians, were aware of the criminal character of the planned campaign. The former German ambassador in Rome, Ulrich von Hassel, made the following notation in his diary in May 1941: *"With this submission to Hitler's orders, Brauchitsch has sacrificed the honor of the German Army."*

The German occupation

The plans drawn up for the territories of the Soviet Union conquered by the German *Wehrmacht* provided for a military administration and a so-called civilian administration.

The military administration was divided into the "battle zone", the "army rear areas", and the three "army group rear areas". Together, these areas included almost two-thirds of the conquered territory. Executive power was in the hands of the commanders of the armies or of the army groups. Commanders of military administration headquarters were responsible for carrying out orders locally.

The civilian administration, which was subordinate to the Ministry for the Occupied Eastern Territories, was established in the areas already "pacified." It was divided into two "Reich Commissariats," the Reich Commissariat *Ostland*, made up of Estonia, Latvia, Lithuania, and the western part of White Russia, and the Reich Commissariat Ukraine, consisting of parts of the Ukraine.

Nazi Party *Gauleiter* were appointed to the highest positions in the civilian administration, and the lower levels were manned by functionaries of the NSDAP as well.

The power of the civilian administration was limited by three other agencies of occupation:
• The *Wehrmacht* Commander (High Command of the *Wehrmacht*) responsible for military security.
• The Economic Staff East (Hermann Göring), responsible for plundering these territories.
• The Security Police and Security Service (SD, Reinhard Heydrich), responsible for fighting the opponents of National Socialism.

The instruments of genocide

The leaders of the SS and the *Wehrmacht* created a variety of instruments aimed at facilitating the execution of planned genocide in these occupied territories:

• Four *Einsatzgruppen* of the SS accompanied the units of the German *Wehrmacht*, as had been the case in Poland. The *Einsatzgruppen*, whose primary task was the murder of Jews, were divided into *Einsatzkommandos* and *Sonderkommandos* and totaled 2,500 men.

• Since 1939, tens of thousands of police had been called up for service in police battalions and police regiments and prepared for battle. In some cases, they were armed with heavy weapons.

• Heinrich Himmler had established three brigades of *Waffen-SS* for direct intervention. These 19,000 men were under his direct command.

• To coordinate these death squads of the police and the SS, higher SS and police leaders were appointed for duty in the areas designated for future military and civilian administration. These men were deputies of Himmler and could also command regular divisions of the *Waffen-SS* as needed for "special tasks."

• For these campaigns of annihilation, the *Wehrmacht* created two special units, the Military Police and the Secret Field Police. The chief task of the former was to regulate troop movements and to maintain discipline, whereas the latter was charged solely with combating political opponents, including Jews.

The regular *Wehrmacht* units, whether advancing in battle or behind the front lines, were involved in the murder of prisoners of war, Jews, "Gypsies", and other segments of the civilian population in many ways. They cooperated with the above-cited commandos of the police and the SS as well as acting on their own initiative.

# Walter Manoschek   Serbia: The War Against the Partisans, 1941

The war year 1941 began with the *Wehrmacht's* invasion of Yugoslavia and Greece. Hitler decided to attack these two countries following the successful military coup against the pro-German Yugoslavian government in late March 1941. The aim was to secure the *Wehrmacht's* southeastern flank for the war already planned against the Soviet Union.

On April 6, German and Italian troops attacked the two southeastern European countries. The war was a classic *Blitzkrieg:* Yugoslavia capitulated on April 18th, Greece three days later.

Greece was divided into various zones of occupation by the victors, but remained intact as a state. The Yugoslavian state, however, was destroyed, its individual regions divided among the Axis partners. In Croatia the Third Reich installed a formally independent satellite state under the leadership of the fascist Ustasha movement. Serbia was governed by the German military until 1944.

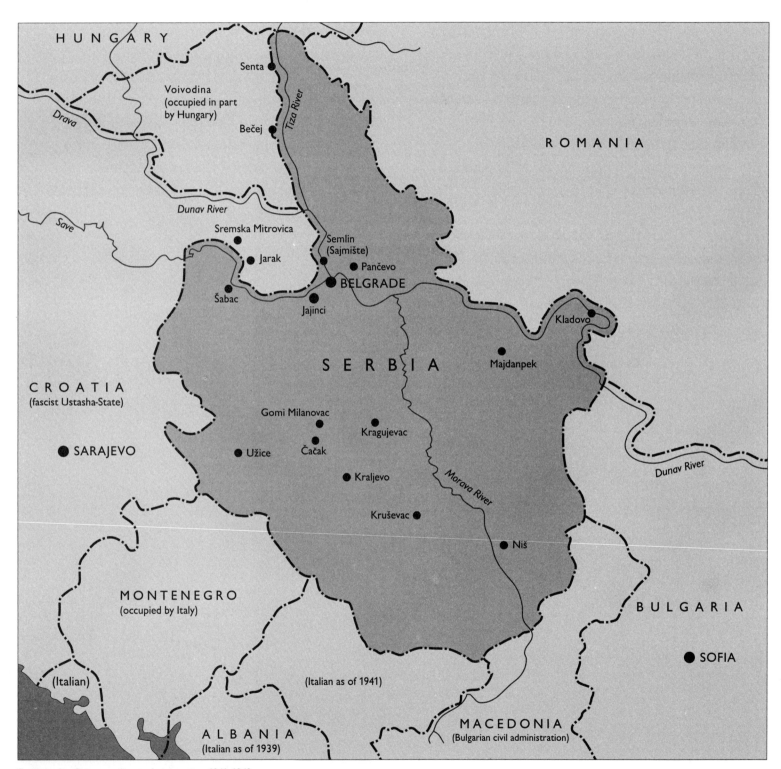

HUNGARY

Voivodina
(occupied in part
by Hungary)

ROMANIA

Drava

Save

Dunav River

Tiza River

Senta

Bečej

Sremska Mitrovica

Jarak

Šabac

Semlin
(Sajmište)

Pančevo

BELGRADE

Jajinci

Kladovo

SERBIA

Majdanpek

CROATIA
(fascist Ustasha-State)

SARAJEVO

Gomi Milanovac

Užice

Čačak

Kragujevac

Kraljevo

Kruševac

Morava River

Dunav River

Niš

MONTENEGRO
(occupied by Italy)

BULGARIA

SOFIA

(Italian)

(Italian as of 1941)

ALBANIA
(Italian as of 1939)

MACEDONIA
(Bulgarian civil administration)

Serbia under German military administration, 1941–1942

From the bombing of Belgrade to the assault on the Soviet Union

"Operation Punishment"

The invasion of Yugoslavia had the code name "Operation Punishment." Serbia, especially, was to be punished. From the beginning, the leadership of the German Army broke the rules of conventional warfare: Yugoslavia was attacked without a declaration of war. More than 600 combat and fighter planes attacked the capital Belgrade, which had no anti-aircraft defenses. Incendiary and fragmentation bombs destroyed large parts of the city. More people were killed in these air attacks than in the previous bombings of Warsaw, Coventry, and Rotterdam combined.

1–3: Buildings in Belgrade destroyed by fragmentation bombs, April 1941.

2

3

## The persecution of the Jews begins

While preparing for the war in the Balkans, the Army High Command and the head of the Reich Security Main Office (*Reichsicherheitshauptamt*, RSHA), Reinhard Heydrich, agreed on the forms of cooperation between the *Wehrmacht* and the special political forces of the RSHA in the occupied territories: *Einsatzgruppen*, mobile units, were to act under the auspices of army formations but "to take executive measures affecting the civilian populations on their own responsibility." This agreement, originally reached for the war against the Soviet Union, was adopted for the Balkans with two crucial points added by Army Chief of Staff Franz Halder: Along with "emigrants, saboteurs, terrorists," the *Einsatzgruppen* of the Security Police and the Security Service were also to "take Communists and Jews into custody."

While Serbian Communists remained relatively unmolested, at least until the invasion of the Soviet Union, because of the existing pact between Hitler and Stalin, persecution of the Jews began immediately. *Wehrmacht* units and German police authorities took the initiative:

As early as three days before the capitulation of Yugoslavia, the local commander of Grossbetschkerek/Zrenjanin ordered Jewish businesses to be marked as such and closed. A few days later his successor ordered that the Star of David be worn, that "reparations" of one million Reich Marks be paid, and that the Jewish community be banished into a ghetto. Simultaneously, the *Einsatzgruppe* in Belgrade ordered the registration of all male Jews in the city. On April 19, 1941, nearly 10,000 Belgrade Jews gathered in the center of Belgrade to be registered by the Gestapo. Supervised by *Wehrmacht* units, they were subjected to forced labor.

On May 31, 1941, the military commander of Serbia, General Ludwig von Schröder, ordered that all Jews be defined and marked as such. Furthermore, he ordered the "Aryanization" of their property and their dismissal from all employment in civil service and the private sector.

Military Administration Headquarters Belgrade
April 25, 1941, Belgrade
Decree

1) All Jews living in Belgrade can buy groceries and other goods in markets and squares only after 10:30 each day. Salespersons may not sell [goods] to them earlier.

2) At public fountains and other places where citizens wait in lines, Jews can join the lines only after all other citizen-Aryans [Bürger-Arier] have received the relevant articles;

3) Salespersons are forbidden to sell groceries and other goods to Jews at higher prices or in any illicit manner;

4) All Jews who disobey this regulation will be punished with up to 30 days arrest or fines up to 10,000 dinar. As seen fit, they may also be sent to concentration camps; salespersons cited in Article 3 will receive the same punishment; and

5) Penalties in keeping with this regulation will be imposed by the police of Belgrade or its boroughs. This regulation takes effect immediately.

Issued on April 25, 1941 in Belgrade.
Colonel and Commanding Officer von Kaisenberg

Letter from the field, Peter G., June 18, 1941

". . . Sometimes one feels sorry for the Jews. There are still loads of them running around here. It is strange, however, that I still haven't met a single racial Jew [Rassejuden]. They can't be distinguished on appearance from the Aryans. In the villages, the Jewish pack is detailed to shovel work, etc. In the morning the rabble has to report for roll call and chant the morning slogan:

" 'We can't even imagine Germany's power and strength!' Pretty good, don't you think? We will soon teach this pack discipline.

"The population's respect for us is uncanny. In any case we are well regarded and liked by everyone. Whether Germans, Hungarians, Serbs, or Romanians . . ."

## "V"—das Zeichen unseres Sieges

### Der Sieg des Guten ueber das Boese. der Ordnung ueber das Chaos, des Aufbauwillens ueber das zerstoerende Element des Judentums

1: From a German military newspaper, July 1941:

"'V' – the sign of our victory. The victory of good over evil, of order over chaos, of the will to build over the destructive element of Jewry"

## An die Juden!

Alle Juden haben gelbe Armbinden zu tragen. Wer sich ohne Armbinde auf der Strasse oder in öffentlichen Lokalen zeigt, wird nach den Kriegsgesetzen bestraft.
Kommandantur Belgrad

## Јеврејима!

Сви Јевреји имају да носе жуте траке око руке. Ко се нађе на улици или у јавном локалу без траке око руке, биће кажњен по ратним законима.
Команда места Београда

2: Regulation for wearing the yellow arm band:

"To the Jews! All Jews must wear yellow arm bands. Whoever appears on the street or in public places without an arm band will be punished according to martial law. Military Administration Headquarters Belgrade"

**Alle Juden haben sich am 19 April d. J. um 8 Uhr morgens bei der Städtischen Schutzpolizei (im Feuerwehrkomando am Taš - Majdan) zu melden.**

**Juden die dieser Meldepflicht nicht nachkommen, werden erschossen.**

Belgrad 16-IV 1941

Der Chef der Einsatzgruppe
der Sicherheitspolizei
und des S. D.

**Сви Јевреји морају да се пријаве 19 априла т. г. у 8 час. у јутро градској полицији (у згради Пожарне команде на Ташмајдану).**

**Јевреји који се не одазову овом позиву биће стрељани.**

Београд, 16-IV-1941 год.

Шеф групе полиције
безбедности и С. Д.

1: Decree concerning the registration of the Jews of Belgrade, April 16, 1941.

"All Jews must register on April 19 of this year at eight a.m. with the Municipal Police (in the fire station at Taš-Majdan). Jews who do not register will be shot. Belgrade, 4/16/1941. Head of the *Einsatzgruppe* of the Security Police and of the S.D."

2–5: Registration of Jews at the fire station in Belgrade, April 19, 1941.

3

4

5

6–7: German and Hungarian soldiers assign Jews from Zemun and Senta to forced labor, May 1941.

7

8: Sign on a streetcar in Belgrade, prohibiting its use by Jews.

The first "atonement measures" against the Serbian population

From the beginning of its occupation of Serbia, the *Wehrmacht* left no doubt that the repressive methods it was willing to employ against the civilian population included actions that were tantamount to war crimes, according to existing international norms. When one German soldier was shot and one seriously wounded in Pančevo, *Wehrmacht* soldiers and the *Waffen-SS* rounded up about 100 civilians at random.

The town commander, Lieutenant Colonel Fritz Bandelow, conducted court martials, which were not in keeping with the norms of military law. The presiding judge, *SS-Sturmbannführer* Rudolf Hofmann, sentenced 36 of those arrested to the death penalty. On April 21, 1941, four of the arrested civilians were the first to be shot. On the following day, eighteen victims, including one woman, were hanged in a cemetery and fourteen more were shot at the cemetery wall by an execution squad of the *Wehrmacht's Großdeutschland Regiment.* The victims' bodies were left hanging for several days as a deterrent.

1–4: Hangings in the Pančevo cemetery, April 22, 1941.

2

4

3

43

1–4: Shootings at the Pančevo cemetery wall, April 22, 1941.

2

3

4

The assault on the Soviet Union on June 22, 1941 brought about a marked change in the politics of military occupation in Serbia. On that date, the leading Communist functionaries and former participants in the Spanish Civil War were arrested. The Jewish community was forced to select 40 men every day who were to be shot as hostages, should attacks on occupation forces or installations occur. The enemy was clearly defined: Communists and Jews.

In early July 1941, the Communist Party of Yugoslavia under the leadership of Tito commenced with their armed struggle against the occupiers. Initially, the police and the Security Service of the SS were assigned the task of fighting the partisans. As the armed resistance of the Serbian partisans spread in the course of the summer, Hitler charged the *Wehrmacht* troops with putting down the insurrection. But because the *Wehrmacht* was not successful in combatting partisan resistance by military means, it turned to other methods: supposed Communists and Jews were shot or publicly hanged as "atonement" [Sühne].

Thus, after an (unsuccessful) attempt to assassinate the German-Austrian General Adalbert Lontschar on July 20, 1941, a total of 52 supposed Communists and Jews from various towns in the area were shot. Among them were numerous victims from Čačak.

In Belgrade, victims were hanged publicly as a "deterrent." In the city of Kruševac, "atonement" and "deterrent" were combined in a special way: After Veselin Nikolić was shot by a *Wehrmacht* execution squad, the dead man's body was subsequently hung up in a public place as a "deterrent." Numerous people were also publicly hanged in Belgrade as a "deterrent."

Through the end of August 1941, 32 *Wehrmacht* soldiers were killed by partisans in Serbia. During the same period, more than 1,000 Communists and Jews were murdered by the *Wehrmacht* and police.

1: *Wehrmacht* soldiers round up hostages to be shot in Čačak, July 20, 1941.

2: *Wehrmacht* men pose with the victims, Čačak, July 20, 1941.

1–5: The shooting of Veselin Nikolić . . .

2

3

4

5

6: . . . and then the public hanging in Kruševac, August 1941.

## Document

Letter from the field, Peter G., August 1941

"Our 'home' radio station, from the Belgrade Propaganda Company, supports the spirit of the capital letter 'V'. During the day and in the evening there's wonderful music. At the beginning of each news report the Belgrade station broadcasts a phrase from Beethoven's 5th Symphony as a special 'V' signal. It sounds beautiful, powerful. Can you receive Belgrade with your radio, every evening they broadcast German news at 8 and 10 p.m.? Maybe you will have a chance to hear it. But don't be shocked if the number of executed Communists or Jews happens to be announced. They are listed daily at the end of the news. Today a record was set! This morning 122 Communists and Jews were executed by us in Belgrade. You might hear my city, Gr. K., mentioned, too. It is often named.

Yesterday the Communists there tried to set fire to (7) different parts of the city. Yesterday more than 30 people were executed. And a few days ago the impudent rabble dared to use hand grenades to smoke out the quarters where soldiers of our regiment were sleeping at night!!! I don't know how many died in the attack . . .

Did you know that my pay (in fact, the pay of the entire *Wehrmacht*!) was raised by 25% as of 7/1/1941? A signal that we will wear these grey uniforms for a long time . . ."

1-7: Public hangings in Belgrade, August 17, 1941.

2

3

50

4

5

6

7

51

The bloody autumn of 1941 in Serbia

In spite of determined repressive measures by the *Wehrmacht* and police, resistance spread steadily throughout Serbia. In September 1941, the Serbian-nationalist Chetniks joined the armed struggle of the partisans. Soon the resistance movement controlled most of the country with the exception of the large cities. While on the Eastern Front the *Wehrmacht* seemed to roll unimpeded toward Moscow, in Serbia it appeared that the weak occupation forces would not be able to hold the country much longer.

On September 16, 1941 Hitler appointed General Franz Böhme Plenipotentiary Commanding General in Serbia, in charge of all military and civilian units and agencies.

It was no accident that Wilhelm Keitel, the Chief of the High Command of the *Wehrmacht*, issued an order that same day aimed at combating the "Communist uprising in the occupied territories" which declared the "death penalty for 50–100 Communists . . . appropriate as atonement for the life of one German soldier." Armed with Keitel's guidelines, General Böhme arrived in Serbia with the assignment "to restore order over the long run in the entire area with the most drastic measures" (Hitler, Führerweisung 31a, September 16, 1941).

The Šabac concentration camp

From the beginning, General Böhme left no doubt that he was planning "punitive actions", not only against the partisans, but against the entire civilian population. First of all, General Böhme ordered the "cleansing" of the Mačva region around the city of Šabac:

"Ruthless measures must create a deterrent that will rapidly become known throughout Serbia. All participants who participate in the struggle in any way are to be seen as irregulars and are to be dealt with as such. All settlements from which or in whose vicinity German troops are fired on or in whose vicinity weapons or munitions are found are to be burned to the ground.

"The entire male population between the ages of 15 and 60 is to be arrested and transported initially to the prisoner collection stations to be established by the division . . . From the first day on, the entire female population is to carry out the same work or be subjected to forced labor."

(General Böhme's order for the "cleansing" of the Mačva region, September 22, 1941)

1–3: Deportation of the civilian population from the Mačva region to the Šabac concentration camp, September 1941.

2

3

General Böhme pointed out the historical dimension of this order to his troops:

"You are to carry out your task in an area in which, in 1914, rivers of German blood flowed as the result of the duplicity of the Serbs, men and women. You are the avengers of these dead. A deterrent must be created for all of Serbia, one that will have the most extreme effect on the entire population. Anyone who is lenient sins against the lives of his fellow-soldiers. Regardless of who he is, he will be held responsible and brought before a court martial."

(General Böhme's instructions to all units, September 25, 1941)

A few days later the 342nd Infantry Division submitted its report on the "cleansing" of Mačva: "830 men from the opposing side were shot and 8,400 prisoners were taken. Captured weapons included only one piece of artillery, 2 machine guns, several rifles with some ammunition, a train vehicle and a motorboat. . . . Health and morale of the troops quite good."

(10-day report of the 342nd Infantry Division to the XVIIIth Army Corps, September 30, 1941)

An improvised outdoor concentration camp was established in Šabac. . All men from the town and from the "cleansed" villages of the Mačva region were rounded up and interned there.

Thousands of prisoners from Šabac and Sremska Mitrovica were brought to Jarak to build a larger concentration camp. The convoy, known as the "Blood March", was escorted by *Wehrmacht* units:

"On this march all who could not continue or who were, from the beginning, too weak for the march were shot on the spot by the escorting *Wehrmacht* detachment."

(Court testimony by a member of the 64th Police-Reserve Battalion, Bruno W., who accompanied this march)

"At 1 p.m. a member of the ethnic-German movement reported to Section Ib that approximately 150 prisoners, who were part of a convoy on route from Mitrovica to Jarak, with an escort of Croatian military units and only a few *Wehrmacht* soldiers, escaped on the road between Mitrovica and Jarak. Approximately 90 of the escapees were said to be lying dead on the road between Mitrovica and Jarak. The rest escaped into the corn fields to the north."

(Daily report of the 342nd Infantry Division, October 1, 1941)

Because the terrain in Jarak proved to be unsuitable for construction of a concentration camp, the survivors of the "Blood March" were driven back to the Šabac concentration camp. In October 1941 the camp was overcrowded with more than 25,000 prisoners.

1: Mountain infantry unit taking part in the "cleansing action" in the Mačva region, September 1941.

3

2–3: The "Blood March" from Šabac to Jarak, September 1941.

5

4–6: Shooting of victims of the "Blood March" by *Wehrmacht* soldiers, September 1941.

6

The imprisoned civilians in Šabac included a group of more than 1,000 Jews from Austria, Berlin, Danzig and Czechoslovakia. They were part of the so-called "Kladovo Transport," a group of Jewish refugees that had left Vienna at the end of 1939 with the aim of traveling by ship down the Danube and across the Black Sea to Palestine. The group was held up in Yugoslavia, and the refugees had been living in Šabac since 1940. Now they too became prisoners of the German and Austrian occupiers.

Together with "Gypsies" also imprisoned there, the Jews of the "Kladovo Transport" were the first prisoners from the Šabac concentration camp to die in the *Wehrmacht's* "hostage shootings".

1: People from the Jewish "Kladovo Transport" being brought to the Šabac concentration camp.

2: Imprisoned "Gypsies" from the Mačva region awaiting deportation to the Šabac concentration camp, September 1941.

3: Groups of "Gypsies" arriving at the Šabac concentration camp, September 1941.

4: Selection of victims to be shot in the Šabac
concentration camp, October 1941. Left foreground:
a *Wehrmacht* sergeant.

5–6: Prisoners in the Šabac concentration camp,
October 1941.

6

1: Vukosova Garilović-Kostić on the way to being shot, Šabac, November 1941.

2: Victims from the Šabac concentration camp on the way to being shot, fall 1941.

3: Shooting operation in Šabac, September 1941.

4: Victims shot on an open field in Šabac, September 26 and 28, 1941.

5: Mass shooting in Šabac, September 26, 1941.

6: Victims of a shooting are buried in pits, Šabac, fall 1941.

7: Two *Wehrmacht* sergeants observe the burial of shooting victims in the vicinity of Šabac, fall 1941.

On October 4, 1941, General Franz Böhme issued his first order to murder Jews. Twenty-one *Wehrmacht* soldiers had died in a skirmish with partisans. General Böhme ordered the shooting of 2,100 "hostages" as "atonement" and stipulated from which groups the victims were to be chosen:

"The head of the military government is requested to select 2,100 prisoners in the concentration camps at Šabac and Belgrade (mainly Jews and Communists)."

For the first time, *Wehrmacht* units were to be responsible for carrying out these mass shootings:

"The shooting squads are to be drawn from the 342nd Division (for the Šabac concentration camp) and from the 449th Corps Signal Battalion (for the concentration camp at Belgrade)."

(Both quotations: General Böhme's order to the quartermaster section of the XVIIIth Army Corps, April 10, 1941)

The men of the "Kladovo Transport" and the "Gypsies" detained in the Šabac concentration camp became the victims of this *Wehrmacht* execution:

"805 Jews and Gypsies are to be taken from the Šabac camp, the rest from the Jewish transit camp in Belgrade."

(SD Operational Situation Report, September 10, 1941)

To arrive at the required number of victims, Serbian civilians interned in the Šabac concentration camp were also shot. One report on the Šabac concentration camp states:

"Total number of prisoners approximately 22,000, about 8,000 checked to date, 910 liquidated to date by the *Wehrmacht*."

(SD Operational Situation Report, October 20, 1941)

On October 10, 1941, General Franz Böhme issued an order that served as the basis for the subsequent *Wehrmacht* massacres of Jews, "Gypsies", and Serbs:

"In all locations in Serbia, all Communists, inhabitants suspected of being such, all Jews, and a certain number of inhabitants with nationalistic and democratic tendencies are to be immediately taken as hostages. These hostages and the population are to be told that the hostages will be shot in the event of attacks on German soldiers or on ethnic Germans."

(Order by General Böhme on the "Suppression of the Communist resistance movement", October 10, 1941)

Between October and December 1941, mass executions by the *Wehrmacht* had become a common practice of the occupation forces in Serbia. In the two last weeks of October alone, more than 9,000 Jews, "Gypsies" and other civilians were shot.

To keep the bureaucracy of the mass murders running smoothly, forms for "Hostage Executions" were printed; now it was merely necessary to type in the date, the incident to be "atoned for," the number of persons to be executed, and the unit assigned to perform the execution.

Liepe.
1st Lieutenant and Company Commander
Local quarters, 10/13/1941
Field post number 26 557
Report on the execution of Jews on 10/9/1941 and 10/11/1941

1. Order:
   Order was given to shoot 2,200 Jews from the camp in Belgrade on 10/8/41.

2. Leadership and participation:
   1st Lieutenant Liepe and soldiers of the Field Units 26 557 and 06 175, of which 2 officers and 20 enlisted men are dead and 16 are missing and 3 are wounded.

3. Medical care and supervision:
   Medical Lieutenant Dr. Gasser, Field Unit 39 107, and Medical Lance Sergeant Bente of Unit 26 557.

4. Transportation and vehicles:
   Transportation and guarding of the prisoners was carried out by the units involved. Vehicles were provided by the motor pool of military administration headquarters in Belgrade. Transportation of the soldiers involved was by army vehicles.

5. Place of action:
   On 10/9/41 – Woods approximately 12 kilometers northeast of Kovin. On 10/11/41 – near the Belgrade shooting range on the road to Niš.

6. Security and cover:
   Carried out in closest cooperation with the Security Police in Belgrade and Pančevo.

7. Film and photography:
   Information & Press Company "S."

8. Supervision:
   1st Lieutenant Liepe, Lieutenant Vibrans, Lieutenant Lüstraeten, SS-Oberscharführer Enge, Security Police Belgrade.

9. Implementation:
   After a thorough examination of the site and careful preparation, the first shootings were carried out on 10/9/1941. The prisoners were picked up with their emergency luggage from the camp in Belgrade at 5:30 a.m. Shovels and other tools were handed out to simulate a work detail. Each vehicle was guarded by only 3 men so that no suspicions about the true activities would be raised by a large number of guards. The transport occurred with no difficulties. The mood of the prisoners during the trip and preparations was good. They were happy to be brought out of the camp, as their quarters there were supposedly not to their liking. The prisoners were given work 8 kilometers from the shooting site and later brought to the site as needed.

The place was suitably secured during preparations and the shootings. The shootings were carried out using rifles at a distance of 12 meters. Five riflemen were ordered to shoot each prisoner. Additionally, two riflemen were at the doctor's disposal, who were to kill prisoners with shots through the head on his orders. Valuables and superfluous items were gathered and later delivered to the N.S.V. [National Socialist People's Welfare] or the Security Police in Belgrade.

The prisoners were calm during the shootings. Two people attempted to escape and were shot immediately. Some expressed their sympathies by shouting praise for Stalin and Russia. On 10/9/41, 180 men were shot. The shooting was concluded at 6:30 p.m. There were no unusual occurrences. The units returned to their quarters satisfied. Because of work on the Danube ferry, the second shooting could not take place until 10/11/41. As a result of that work, the next shooting took place in the vicinity of Belgrade. It was therefore necessary to find a new site. The next shooting took place on 10/11/41 in the vicinity of the shooting range. It proceeded as planned. 269 men were executed. No prisoner escaped during either shooting and the troops had no unusual occurrences or incidents to report. A detachment from the Major Pongruber Unit under the leadership of Second Lieutenant Hau was called in for increased security. On 10/9/41 and 10/11/41, a total of 449 men were shot by the afore-stated units. Unfortunately, due to other deployment orders, an additional shooting by the afore-mentioned units had to be canceled and the task passed on to the Major Pongruber Unit.

Signature (Liepe)
1st Lieutenant and Company Commander

1. Printed form for "Hostage Executions" dated November 20, 1941 and referring to the execution of 385 hostages from the Šabac concentration camp.

## General Franz Böhme: A Biography

| | | | |
|---|---|---|---|
| Born: | April 15, 1885 in Zeltweg, Austria | February 1938: | Designated Chief of the Austrian General Staff at Hitler's request |
| 1900 – 1904: | Enrolled in the Cadet Corps in Graz | 1939 – 1940: | As Commander of the 32nd Division, participation in the war against Poland; Polish Campaign: Deputy Commanding General of the IInd Army Corps |
| 1904 – 1911: | Lieutenant in the 95th Rifle Regiment in Lemberg (Galicia), Ragusa and Cattaro (Dalmatia) | | |
| 1911 – 1914: | War Academy in Vienna | | |
| 1914 – 1918: | General Staff Officer in various units, including the 132nd Infantry Brigade in the German Army South and on the staff of the 51st German Corps Headquarters for special duty | April – Sept. 1941: | Commanding General of the XVIIIth Mountain Army Corps in Greece |
| | | Sept. – Dec. 1941: | Plenipotentary Commanding General in Serbia |
| 1920: | Joins the Austrian Army | June – July 1944: | As the Commander in Chief of the 2nd Panzer Army, Commander of the German troops in Yugoslavia |
| 1921 – 1935: | General Staff Officer and Chief of Staff in various brigades | | |
| 1929: | Colonel of the General Staff | July 1944: | Serious injury in a plane crash |
| 1935 – 1938: | Head of the Military Counter-Intelligence Service in the Austrian National Ministry of Defense | Jan. – May 1945: | Commander of the 20th Mountain Army and *Wehrmacht* Commander North in Norway |
| 1936: | Brigadier General [Generalmajor] | | |

| | |
|---|---|
| May 10, 1947: | Defendant in Military Court V of the USA (Subsequent Nuremberg Trials, "Hostages Case") in Nuremberg. Together with 11 other high-ranking *Wehrmacht* officers stationed in Yugoslavia and Greece, Franz Böhme is accused of war crimes and crimes against humanity |
| May 29, 1947: | Franz Böhme commits suicide in prison |

1: Franz Böhme as a recruit in the Ritter von Rodakowski 95th Infantry Regiment in Lemberg, 11/1/1905 (seated, extreme left)

2: Colonel Franz Böhme during staff officer training in Linz, March/April 1933.

3: Lieutenant Franz Böhme on leave, 1907.

4: Brigadier General Franz Böhme after being designated Chief of the Austrian General Staff of the Austrian Army, February 1938.

5: Franz Böhme as a General of the German *Wehrmacht*.

The massacre in Kraljevo

In early October 1941, partisan and Chetnik units controlled most of Serbia's countryside. The *Wehrmacht* withdrew from southern Serbia. A total of 1,400 men of the Infantry Regiments 749 and 737 of the 717th Infantry Division occupied the town of Kraljevo. Since the town's railway car factory and airplane motor factory were needed for the German war economy, the city was to be defended at all costs.

The partisans and Chetniks had been attacking Kraljevo with artillery since early October. On October 13, the *Wehrmacht* units in Kraljevo were surrounded by opposing forces. The next day, *Wehrmacht* units arrested "Communists, nationalists, democrats, and Jews – as many as can be guarded – as hostages."

(Daily Report of the 717th Infantry Division, October 14, 1941)

They were to be the first to be shot.

On October 15, a laconic entry in the War Journal reads: "At about 6 p.m. shots from houses, 300 Serbs shot."

(Daily Report of the 717th Infantry Division, October 15, 1941)

On October 16, 1941, soldiers of the 717th Infantry Division were awarded twenty Iron Cross Medals, 2nd Class. That same day, members of the 717th Infantry Division arrested all males in Kraljevo between the ages of 14 and 60 and drove them into the railroad car factory. There they were registered and then led out of the factory in groups of 100 men and shot with machine guns.

On this day, members of the 749th and 737th Infantry Regiments of the 717th Infantry Division executed a total of 1,736 men and 19 "Communist women."

The Commander of the 717th Infantry Division, General Hoffmann, was extremely satisfied with his troops' accomplishments in Kraljevo: "The battles to relieve and supply the Kraljevo post which took place between 10/13/41 and 10/21/41 have, to a certain extent, reached their conclusion since we have fulfilled our goals. The high demands (difficult battle conditions, marches, bivouacs, weather conditions) which our troops faced were met fully and with great enthusiasm. Heavy losses were inflicted on our opponents!"

(Division Order of the day, Number 39, October 23, 1941)

Days earlier, in a personal order of the day, Böhme had expressed his praise as a soldier for the *Wehrmacht* units committing murder in Kraljevo:

"Additional successes recently achieved by the troops serve to further strengthen the reputation of the German *Wehrmacht* in Serbia . . .

"On 10/15, the attack on Kraljevo, which the rebels had been preparing for days, was repulsed by the troops stationed in the town together with the First Battalion of Infantry Regiment 737 advancing from Kruševac. Enemy losses included at least 80 dead; 1,755 hostages were shot as atonement for our losses . . .

"I express my admiration to all officers, non-commissioned officers, and enlisted men who were engaged in these successful operations. Onward to new deeds! Böhme."

(Order of the day from General Böhme, October 20, 1941)

1: *Wehrmacht* officers during a briefing in Kraljevo, early October 1941.

2: *Wehrmacht* soldiers secure a battered truck in Kraljevo, October 1941.

3: Train wreck due to the destruction of tracks in Kraljevo, October 1941.

4: Recovery of a wounded or dead *Wehrmacht* soldier in Kraljevo, October 1941.

The Plenipotentiary Commanding General in Serbia
Local Quarters, 10/20/41
Order of the Day

Additional successes recently achieved by the troops serve to further strengthen the reputation of the German *Wehrmacht* in Serbia.

After cleansing the Mačva region the 342nd Infantry Division attacked the enemy in the Cer Mountains. Rebels losses totaled approximately 1,700 dead and 4,500 prisoners. 2 artillery pieces, a number of machine guns, rifles, and ammunition were captured. In Loznica and Koviljača, 40 wounded fellow soldiers were liberated.

Infantry Regiment 125 cleansed the area around Ub and southeast of Obrenovac. Enemy losses in that area number approximately 300 dead.

Detachments of the 704th Infantry Division eased the pressure on the Valjevo post through repeated sorties. Thanks to repeated sorties from the post by detachments of the 717th Infantry Division, the necessary detonations of captured ammunition in the vicinity of Kraljevo could be carried out.

On 10/15, the attack on Kraljevo, which the rebels had been preparing for days, was repulsed by the troops stationed in the city together with the First Battalion of Infantry Regiment 737 advancing from Kruševac. Enemy losses included at least 80 dead, 1,755 hostages were executed as atonement for our losses. In order to realize a further atonement measure, Third Battalion of Infantry Regiment 749 fought its way through multiple skirmishes at numerous roadblocks from Kragujevac to Grn. Milanovac and back. 133 hostages were taken.

I express my admiration to all officers, noncommissioned officers, and enlisted men who were engaged in these successful operations.

Onward to new deeds!

Signature (Böhme)

1: Men from Kraljevo are driven into the railroad car factory, October 16, 1941.

2: Victims are brought in groups from the railroad car factory to the shooting site, October 16, 1941.

3: After the execution a *Wehrmacht* private shoots survivors in the head, October 16, 1941.

4: *Wehrmacht* soldiers guard the bodies of the shooting victims, October 16, 1941.

5: Victims of the massacre in Kraljevo, October 1941.

"Onward to new deeds!": The massacre in Kragujevac

A few days after the massacre in Kraljevo, other units of the 749th and the 724th Infantry Regiments in the town of Kragujevac, only 60 kilometers from Kraljevo, perpetrated a further mass murder of Serbian civilians. After *Wehrmacht* units suffered losses of 10 dead and 26 wounded in fighting with partisans in the vicinity of Kragujevac, they sought 2,300 victims for execution – according to the quota of 100:1 for every soldier killed and 50:1 for every soldier wounded. On October 19, 1941, two battalions fanned out into the neighboring villages and shot "422 male persons on site in the villages with no casualties of our own."

(Letter of the District Commander of Kragujevac, Captain Bischofshausen, to Military Administration Headquarters 610 and to the Commander-in-Chief in Serbia, October 20, 1941)

On the next day, the murders continued in the town of Kragujevac, which numbered approximately 42,000 inhabitants. By order of the Commander of Infantry Regiment 749, Major Otto Desch, *Wehrmacht* soldiers dragged men and boys out of homes, workplaces, and stores or arrested them on the street. Entire school classes were brought with their teachers from schools and incarcerated in a barracks. When, on the evening of October 20, the two *Wehrmacht* units had collected the necessary number of victims, they began the executions:

"10/20. In the evening the Communists and Jews arrested on 10/18 and 53 criminals from the local prison are shot behind the salvage depot for captured materiel."

Next morning, the *Wehrmacht* units continued the massacre by shooting the people incarcerated in the barracks: "10/21. At 7 a.m. the selection and shooting of those arrested begins. This concludes the operation, a total of 2,300 Serbs of various ages and occupations were shot."

(Both quotations: Report of the First Battalion of Infantry Regiment 724, 10/7–10/25/1941)

In the course of a few days, units of the 717th and 704th Infantry Divisions murdered more than 4,000 people in the two largest massacres of civilians in the Balkans. General Böhme's staff noted in the War Journal that the "successful undertakings of the divisions of the LXVth Army Corps indicate a gratifying increase in the aggressive spirit and in the initiative of the troops that have, to date, no doubt tended to passivity."

(War Journal, Operations Section, XVIIIth Mountain Army Corps, 10/23/1941)

Infantry Regiment 724
Local Quarters 10/27/41
Report of the First Battalion of Infantry Regiment 724
for the period 10/17–10/25/1941

I.  General remarks:
    During the absence of the Third Battalion of Infantry
    Regiment 749 (atonement operation in Milanovac),
    the Battalion performed all the guard duty of the post,
    at a strength of 0:21:201. The remainder of the Com-
    pany were given duty as escort squads or as scouts in
    the close vicinity. Great demands were made on
    members of the Battalion in this period. On 10/26/41
    the Third Battalion of Infantry Regiment 749 took
    over all guard duty at the post. With the arrival of a
    company of the Neditsch movement in Kragujevac
    the Battalion received substantial support in the battle
    against Communist bands. These people have demon-
    strated exceptional zeal and nerve and have already
    achieved substantial success in the battle against these
    gangs. The activities of the Communist bands have
    subsided greatly with the onset of bad weather.

II. Specific details:
    The railway tracks between Kragujevac and Lapovo
    and the roads to Kragujevac have been repeatedly
    damaged by bands.

10/17/41:
Railway between Jovanovac and Milanovac disrupted
in several places. 2 squads are protecting those working to repair the tracks. 2 further squads are sent to
inspect the bridge near Petrovac. The inspections
showed that, in the course of the attack on the
bridge, an aerial bomb of approximately 150 kg did
not detonate. It was detonated by an ordnance
specialist of Ordnance Battalion 18.

10/18/41:
The tracks to Lapovo are again blown up in several
places. As much as 30 meters of tracks were torn up
and thrown down the embankment. In the evening 66
Communists and Jews registered in our lists were
arrested and brought to the salvage depot.

According to Division orders, the 9 dead and 26
wounded of the Third Battalion of Infantry Regiment
749 must be avenged. Therefore, the appropriate
numbers of the male population will be taken
prisoner and shot from 10/19–10/21.

10/19/41:
The First Battalion of Infantry Regiment 724 carries
out the operation in Grosnica with 3 companies
and 50 men of Ordnance Battalion 18. 245 men are
shot and the village burned to the ground. Ammunition was found in several places, including in the
church tower.

The Third Battalion of Infantry Regiment 724 shot
182 men in Mackovac.

10/20/41:
Approximately 3,200 men from Kragujevac between
the ages of 16 and 50 are arrested. In the evening the
Communists and Jews arrested on 10/18 and 53
criminals from the local prison in Kragujevac are shot
behind the salvage depot for captured material.

10/21/41:
At 7 a.m. the selection and shooting of those
arrested begins.

This concludes the operation, a total of 2,300 Serbs
of various ages and occupations were shot. For the
next few days there is, understandably, intense unrest
among the population. Consequently, security
measures are taken.

Protecting the town against attacks is now at the
center of attention. Security zones are assigned to
the company and positions are being improved.

10/22/41:
An officer of the Neditsch movement reports that
bands intend to attack Kragujevac tonight. Nothing
happens, however.

10/23/41:
The Third Battalion of Infantry Regiment 749 relieves
all guards at 1200 hours. The battalion thus has no
guard duties except for guarding the Artillery
Barracks and 6 night patrols. At 1400 hours there is a
report that a detachment of the Neditsch movement
came upon a large band near Grosnica and was unable
to hold out. At 1430 hours a platoon led by Second
Lieutenant Günther, Second Company, is sent out in
3 trucks to relieve the Neditsch people. The gang
then withdrew, leaving behind 3 dead. Our losses:
none, 3 wounded among the Neditsch supporters.

The following days (10/24 and 25) are taken up with
machine-gun instruction and improvement of positions for the defense of Kragujevac. On 10/25/41 the
entire battalion is assembled on the parade grounds
of the artillery barracks for a briefing on the events
of the preceding days.

Signature (König)
Major and Battalion Commander

STANDORTKOMMANDANTUR
KRAGUJEVAC     *Kragujevac, den 21. Oktober 1941.*

## Bekanntmachung

Die feigen und hinterlistigen Ueberfälle in der vergangenen Woche auf deutsche Soldaten, wobei 10 getötet und 26 verwundet wurden, mussten gesühnt werden.

Es wurden deshalb für jeden getöteten deutschen Soldaten 100 und für jeden verwundeten 50 Landesbewohner u. zw. vor allem Kommunisten, Banditen und deren Helfershelfer, zusammen 2.300, erschossen.

In Zukunft wird bei jedem ähnlichen Fall, sei es auch nur ein Sabotageakt, mit gleicher Strenge durchgegriffen werden.

*Der Standortälteste.*

МЕСНА КОМАНДАНТУРА
КРАГУЈЕВАЦ     *Крагујевац, 21. Октобра ·1941.*

## ОБЗНАНА

Кукавички и подмукли препади у току про уле недеље на немачке војника којом приликом је погинуло 10 а рањено 26 немачких војника морали су бити кажњени.

Због тога је за сваког погинулог немачко војника стрељано 100, а за сваког рањеног 50 становника и то пре свега комуниста, бандита њихових помагача, укупно 2300.

У будуће ће се за сваки сличан случај, па било то само саботажа, поступити са истом строгошћу.

*Старешина месне Команде*

"Post Headquarters Kragujevac, October 21, 1941—Announcement

The cowardly and insidious attacks on German soldiers last week, in which 10 were killed and 26 wounded, must be atoned. For every German soldier killed, 100 local inhabitants will be shot, for every soldier wounded, 50 will be shot. A total of 2,300 persons will be selected, primarily Communists, bandits and their accomplices. In every similar case in the future, even in cases involving only sabotage, equally drastic measures will be taken.

Post Commander"

1–8: Stari Bečej (Vojvodina): On November 11, 1941, 11 young people were shot as "atonement" by a unit of the Hungarian Army, which was allied with the *Wehrmacht*. Among the victims were Milan Gavrić (photo 2, saying goodbye to his mother), Toša Cvejanov and Stevan Kojić (photo 1, saying goodbye to his father).

2

3

4

5

6

7

8

By the time General Böhme was recalled from his post in Serbia on December 6, 1941 after scarcely three months of duty, his troops had run up a murderous "balance sheet":

The German tally of 160 dead and 278 wounded soldiers contrasted with 20,000 to 30,000 civilians who had been shot, including all the adult male Jews in the country.

The Jewish women and children were taken to the Šajmiste-Semlin concentration camp near Belgrade in December 1941 by police and the Security Service. As a military pretext for their internment, the counter-intelligence detachment of the Army High Command 12 in Saloniki declared: "All Jews and Gypsies are to be transferred to a concentration camp near Semlin . . . It has been proven that they were involved in intelligence operations for the rebels."

(Remarks on the occasion of the Deputy Commander-in-Chief's trip to Belgrade, 12/5/1941)

These Jewish women and children, approximately 6,000 in number, were gassed in the spring of 1942 in the Šajmiste-Semlin concentration camp in a "special car", a truck equipped for this purpose and sent from Berlin.

The Plenipotentiary Commanding
General in Serbia
Local Quarters, 12/5/41
Order of the day

The Führer and Supreme Commander of the *Wehrmacht* has called the Staff of XVIIIth Mountain Army Corps to new tasks outside Serbia. As I depart, I express my thanks and my appreciation to all the troops and agencies who have served under me for their accomplishments in the struggle against the Communists and for their efforts to pacify the country. The uprising was crushed in a short time by German troops, supported by Air Force and Navy units. In often tenacious battles against an insidious enemy and in spite of inclement weather conditions and difficult terrain, we have achieved successes which all officers, non-commissioned officers, and enlisted men can recall with pride.

Similarly, I express my thanks and my appreciation to the military administration and to all German civilian agencies for their tireless devotion to duty. The tireless and fine work of these agencies was always carried out in exemplary cooperation with the troops.

Onward to new deeds: Long live the Führer:

(sig.) Böhme
General of the Infantry

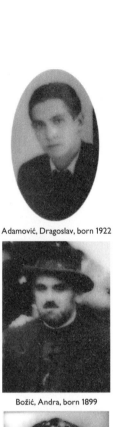

Adamović, Dragoslav, born 1922

Ajvas-Bećir, Begov, born 1914

Aleksić, Nikola, born 1911

Andrejević, Milovan, born 1912

Belajaković, Petar, born 1904

Berger, Livja, born 1911

Božić, Andra, born 1899

Bukumirović, Rajko, born 1920

Ćirjanić, Jevrem, born 1895

Ćorić, Stevo, born 1911

Cvetić, Radislav, born 1892

Cvetković, Života, born 1908

Damnjanivić, Svetozar, born 1900

Dimitrijević, Dušan, born 1921

Djordjević, Kosta, born 1897

Eli, David, born 1899

Eli, Moša, born 1897

Gavrilović, Ljubiša, born 1910

Joksimović, Miodrag, born 1888

Kalafatić, Jovan, born 1911

Lazarević, Jovan, born 1899

Ljubomirović, Ljubomir, born 1911

Milošević, Kostadin, born 1923

Milovanović, Dragiša, born 1911

Naumović, Nada, born 1922

Negovanović, Ljubiša, born 1907

Nikolić, Nikola, born 1892

Novaković, Miodrag, born 1910

Obradović, Milan, born 1916

Orašanin, Andra, born 1902

Pavlović, Dragutin, born 1920     Petljanski, Milorad, born 1924     Petrović, Ljubiša, born 1919     Plemić, Kosta, born 1911     Prokić, Ljubomir, born 1924     Prokić, Miloje, born 1906

Radojčić, Tanasije, born 1897     Radosavljević, Budimir, born 1925     Radosavljević, Živojin, born 1915     Rebić, Ignjat, born 1890     Ristić, Aleksandar, born 1915     Savić, Ljubomir, born 1912

Savkić, Milan, born 1912     Simić Aleksandar, born 1924     Simić, Radislav, born 1914     Simonović, Borivoje, born 1904     Stamenković, Nikola, born 1902     Stojanović, Miodrag, born 1922

Štošić, Krsta, born 1924     Sudimac, Miroslav, born 1904     Tasić, Milutin, born 1914     Tenić, Janko, born 1907     Trajković, Dragomir, born 1899     Trbojević, Milan, born 1899

Vasović, Bogoljub, born 1914     Veljković, Jovan, born 1868     Veljković, Milica, born 1896     Veličković, Miroslav, born 1906     Vilimonović, Miodrag, born 1905     Vulović, Dragoljub, born 1902

Bernd Boll and Hans Safrian **The Sixth Army on the Way to Stalingrad, 1941–1942**

The 6th Army entered the Soviet Union as part of the Army Group South.

The Army High Command 6 (AOK 6), headed by Field Marshal von Reichenau, controlled between 13 and 20 infantry divisions, with exact numbers varying in the course of the year 1941. These divisions penetrated a northern strip of the Ukraine and took the cities Luts'k and Dubno (end of June), Zhytomyr (July), Kiev (September) and Kharkov (end of October). The 6th Army took up winter quarters in the region around Kharkov and Belgorod and began the offensive against Stalingrad in late June 1942.

The 6th Army not only waged war against the military forces of the enemy. Army troops killed groups of prisoners of war and civilians who were declared to be partisans or saboteurs. The Army cooperated with the mobile killing units of the SS, the detachments of the *Einsatzgruppe C.*

The plundering of the Ukraine left large parts of the civilian population in the occupied areas to die of starvation.

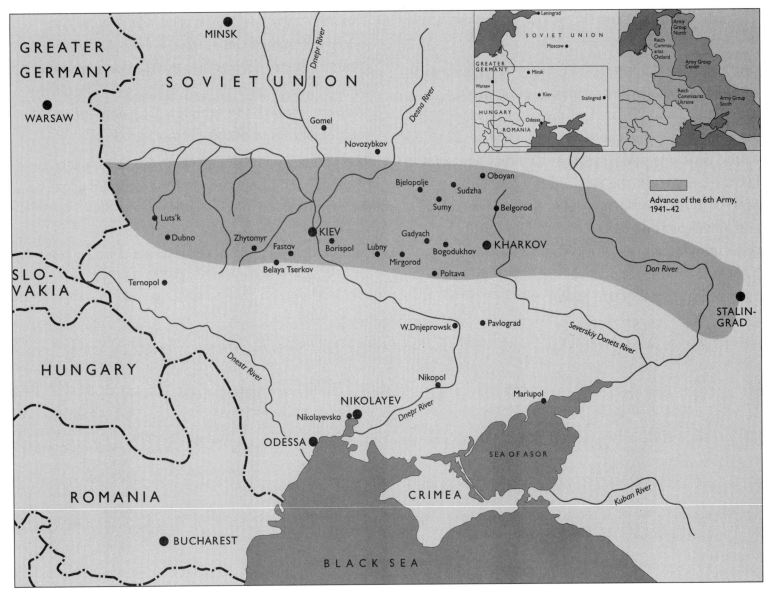

GREATER
GERMANY

● WARSAW

SOVIET UNION

● MINSK

Dnepr River

● Gomel

Desna River

● Novozybkov

● Oboyan

Bjelopolje ● ● Sudzha

● Sumy

● Belgorod

● Luts'k

● Dubno ● Zhytomyr ● Fastov
● Belaya Tserkov

● KIEV
● Borispol ● Lubny

● Gadyach

● Bogodukhov ● KHARKOV

● Mirgorod

● Poltava

SLO-
VAKIA

● Ternopol

Don River

STALIN-
GRAD ●

HUNGARY

Dnestr River

● W.Dnjeprowsk ● Pavlograd

Severskiy Donets River

● Nikopol

● NIKOLAYEV

● Nikolayevsko

Dnepr River

● Mariupol

● ODESSA

SEA OF ASOR

ROMANIA

CRIMEA

Kuban River

● BUCHAREST

BLACK SEA

Leningrad ●

SOVIET UNION

Moscow ●

GREATER
GERMANY

● Minsk

Warsaw ●

● Kiev

● Stalingrad

HUNGARY

Odessa ●

ROMANIA

Army
Group
North

Reich
Commis-
ariat
Ostland

Army
Group
Center

Reich
Commisariat
Ukraine

Army Group
South

Advance of the 6th Army,
1941–42

Ukraine: Operational territory of the 6th army, 1941 – 1942.

Orders issued before the campaign began – the "Decree of Jurisdiction", the "Commissar Order", and the "Guidelines for the Conduct of the Troops in Russia" – defined parts of the civilian population and of the Red Army as enemies who were to be killed at will, including irregulars, political commissars, Communists, and other "hostile civilians" who opposed the *Wehrmacht* or incited others to do so. The troops were generally authorized to kill such persons without specific orders. In the case of civilians who were merely under suspicion of having committed a hostile deed, the nearest officer decided whether they were to live or die.

From the outset, the troops exceeded the actual letter of these orders without being instructed to do so. They executed civilians, for the most part Communists and Jews, in reprisal for ambushes, unsolved cases of sabotage, and similar acts. As early as the beginning of July, even the suspicion of hostile tendencies sufficed. Red Army soldiers who happened to find themselves behind the often obscure front lines when taken prisoner were executed as partisans; Jewish men, who were judged to be supporters of guerrillas and saboteurs, faced the same fate.

**Merkblatt**

**Sieh' Dich vor!**

**Nach Bekanntgabe an die Truppe zu vernichten.**

Der Sowjetfeind, den wir schlagen, hat in allen Kriegen, die er geführt hat, heimtückische und unvorstellbar grausame Methoden angewandt, wie sie dem Charakter des Bolschewismus entsprechen. Die Methoden kennen, heisst gegen sie gewappnet sein. Höchstes Misstrauen ist überall am Platze. Stelle Dich u. a. auf folgende Arten der sowjetischen Kampfführung ein, die Dich nicht überraschen dürfen, und Du wirst dann die Mittel und Wege finden, sie unschädlich zu machen:

1. Gaskrieg in jeder Form. Verseuchung von Rückzugstrassen auf langer Strecke. — Die Gasmaske schützt gegen alle Kampfstoffe. Die Vergeltung ist vorbereitet.

2. Vergiftung von Brunnen, zurückgelassenen Lebensmitteln und Viehbeständen. — Trinke nicht aus Brunnen, sei vorsichtig im Gebrauch von Lebensmitteln, ehe ein Arzt sie geprüft hat.

3. Vermischung von Saatkorn und Gift. Bakterienkrieg (Pest, Cholera, Typhus). Die vorbereiteten sanitätsdienstlichen Massnahmen (Impfen) schützen Dich dagegen. Aber nimm auch Du nichts Essbares von Landeseinwohnern an.

4. Fallschirmabsprung von Saboteuren in Zivil. — Gerade im rückwärtigen Kampfgebiet gilt es, solche Verbrecher sofort unschädlich zu machen, ehe sie unabsehbaren Schaden (Vernichtung von Betriebsstofflagern, Brücken usw.) anrichten.

5. Totstellen und Händehochheben roter Soldaten, dann Wiederaufnahme des Kampfes von rückwärts. — Sofortige Erledigung solcher Gegner ist Dein gutes Recht.

6. Hinterhältiges Anschiessen kleiner Abteilungen und einzelner Leute. Nächtliche Überfälle auf Posten und rückwärtige Kolonnen. — Sei stets bei Tag und Nacht abwehrbereit zum Niederkämpfen solchen Gegners.

7. Verwendung von Viehherden und Einwohnern als Deckung von roten Truppen und Freischärlern. — Betritt nicht vertrauensselig harmlos scheinende Dörfer, ehe sie nicht als feindfrei erkundet sind.

8. Beschiessen erleuchteter Fenster. — Verdunkele sofort, wenn Du Licht anmachen musst.

9. Kraftfahrzeugfallen. — Sorgfältige Erkundung und vorsichtiges Fahren werden Dich vor Überraschungen schützen und die Hindernisse überwinden helfen.

10. Sadistische Behandlung Gefangener. — **Jeder deutsche Soldat muss wissen, dass Gefangenschaft in den Händen der roten Armee gleichbedeutend ist mit grausamen Quälereien und Tod!**

"Watch out!" Flyers like this were used by *Wehrmacht* leaders to prepare the troops for the war against the Soviet Union. The enemy's methods were described as "insidious" and "unimaginably cruel." The German soldiers were called on to exercise caution and confront the enemy with mistrust, brutal reprisals, and the will to fight to the bitter end.

(Source: Bundesarchiv/ Militärarchiv Freiburg)

"Retribution for atrocities"

*Sonderkommando 4 a* – a sub-unit of *Einsatzgruppe C*, consisting of approximately 70 police officers and members of the SD – perpetrated mass murder of the Jewish population. At first, the victims were almost exclusively Jewish men. Usually, Jewish residents of a place just captured were accused of having committed "atrocities" against Ukrainians or captured *Wehrmacht* soldiers. The *Sonderkommando* then executed thousands of Jewish men in "retribution", often assisted by *Wehrmacht* units and Ukrainian "auxiliary volunteers."

Document

299th Infantry Division, Intelligence Section, to the XIXth Army Corps/Intelligence Section, Daily Report, 6/24/1941

"Many irregulars have again appeared in Lokacze. Activity of the irregulars is especially intense in areas settled by Jews."

Document

168th Infantry Division, Intelligence Section, Report 6/22-6/30/1941

"The first act of sabotage reported to Intelligence Section was on 6/25/41 in Ivanitsa where approximately 30 meters of the division telephone line were cut... Because the perpetrators could not be ascertained, retribution measures were carried out by shooting one Jew and one other inhabitant of Ivanitsa who had been a leader of the Communist Party."

Luts'k

Immediately after occupying the town of Luts'k in Wolhynia in late June 1941, the *SD Kommando* rounded up Jews and Communists supposedly responsible for pillage and looting in the town. The 300 Jews and 20 "looters" arrested during the search were shot on June 30.

A proclamation posted in Luts'k in cooperation with officials from the 6th Army ordered all able-bodied Jews to gather at a stated place on July 2 with tools for excavation work. Members of the SS, Order Police, and *Wehrmacht* infantry murdered the more than 1,000 men who obeyed the summons.

Document

Letter from the field, sent from Luts'k by Major Hans Sch., Staff, Engineer Battalion 652, 7/11/1941

"On 7/2 we take over the equipment of our other bridge-building columns in Luts'k ... 1,000 Jews are shot in the old citadel on this day. This is an act of retribution for the 2,800 Ukrainians executed during the Bolshevist period. In return, 5,800 Russians lose their lives. Two officers whom I sent to look for wire and hardware reported that the Jews died without making any sound. After these measures, no doubt regrettable from a humanitarian standpoint but absolutely necessary as a deterrent in the face of rampant activity on the part of the irregulars, we observe that on the next day many of the looters simply set their stolen goods out on the street."

Document

Head of the Security Police and the Security Service, Operational Situation Report USSR Number 24, 7/16/1941

"After the corpses of a total of 10 German *Wehrmacht* soldiers had been discovered on 7/2, 1,160 Jews were shot with the help of a platoon of Order Police and an infantry platoon, in reprisal for the murder of German soldiers and Ukrainians."

2: Columns of prisoners.

4: Rest break.

1–7: Entry into the Ukraine from the perspective of a photographer of the Propaganda Company.

3: Ukrainian women offer refreshments.

5: Cutting the beard of a Jewish man.

6: Briefing.

7: Camouflage in the field.

## Tarnopol'

*Sonderkommando 4 b* purposely incited anti-Jewish pogroms in Tarnopol' in early July 1941. The exhumed corpses of Ukrainians and 10 German soldiers who had been killed by the NKVD were presented to *Wehrmacht* soldiers as victims of the Jews.

"Tarnopol', 7/6/1941.
Dearest Parents!

I have just returned from the laying out of our fellow soldiers from the Air Force and the mountain troops who were captured by the Russians. I can't find the words to describe something like this. Our fellow-soldiers are bound, ears, tongues, nose and genitals have been cut off, that is how we found them in the basement of the Tarnopol' courthouse, and we also found 2,000 Ukrainians and ethnic Germans similarly maltreated. That is Russia and the Jews, the paradise of the worker... Revenge was quick to follow. Yesterday we and the SS were merciful, for every Jew we found was shot immediately. Today things have changed, for we again found 60 fellow-soldiers mutilated. Now the Jews must carry the dead out of the basement, lay them out nicely, and then they are shown the atrocities. After they have seen the victims, they are killed with clubs and spades.

So far, we have sent about 1,000 Jews into the hereafter, but that is far too few for what they have done. The Ukrainians have said that the Jews had all the leadership positions and, together with the Soviets, had a regular public festival while executing the Germans and Ukrainians. I ask you, dear parents, to make this known, also father, in the local branch [of the NSDAP]. If there should be doubts, we will bring photos with us. Then there will be no doubts.

Many greetings, your son Franzl."

(Letter from the field from Tarnopol')

Document

Operational Situation Report, USSR Number 28, 7/20/1941

"The troops passing through, who had the opportunity to see these horrors and, above all, the corpses of the murdered German soldiers, beat a total of about 600 Jews to death and set fire to their houses.

"The following units passed through Tarnopol' in early July 1941: SS Viking Division, 9th Armored Division, 60th Infantry Division, 125th Infantry Division."

1–4: The pogrom in Tarnopol'.

2

3

4

## Zhytomyr

In early August 1941, the SD arrested two officials of a Soviet regional court, Kieper and Kogan. They were tortured until they admitted committing "atrocities." At the same time, the SD, supported by the *Wehrmacht* post headquarters, arrested more than 400 Jewish men in Zhytomyr.

On August 7, 1941, a car with a loudspeaker belonging to the 6th Army Propaganda Company (PK 637) drove through the town and announced in both German and Ukrainian a public execution in the marketplace. More than 400 Jewish men guarded by the SS sat next to a gallows. Among the hundreds of onlookers were numerous *Wehrmacht* soldiers.

"The guards asked the people standing there if someone had business to settle with anyone. Then Ukrainians spoke up who accused this or that Jew of some offense or other. While still in a seated position, these Jews were then beaten and kicked and otherwise mistreated, mostly by Ukrainians."

Finally, Kieper and Kogan were stood on the bed of a truck and hanged.

"[T]he soldiers[*Landser*] who were watching shouted 'slowly, slowly,' so they could take better photographs."

(Quotations: testimony of former soldiers P. A. and J., *Landeskriminalamt Nordrhein-Westfalen* February 27, 1964 and January 26, 1966)

1–6: At the marketplace in Zhytomyr, August 7, 1941

2

3

4

5

6

After Kieper and Kogan had been hanged, the SD took the 400 Jews out of town and shot them in the presence of members of the General Staff of the 6th Army.

Testimony of Dr. A. N., a former colonel on the court-martial committee, Army High Command 6, *Landeskriminalamt Nordrhein-Westfalen*, 10/8/1965.

"A bit away from the road, I then saw a group of people . . . When I arrived there, I found the following scene: A pit had been dug measuring between 10 and 15 meters in length and about 4 meters wide. At a distance of about 15 meters stood a row – or double row – of members of a SS unit. Each time, 10 to 12 natives were led to this pit, stood with their faces to the pit and with their backs to the SS riflemen and were then shot on command by the SS riflemen. They immediately fell into the pit . . . Other members of the staff were there as well . . . During supper in the casino – presumably before and after the actual supper – this incident was discussed, since, as it turned out, a large number of the members of the staff had watched. We all expressed our uneasiness regarding these events. It was also mentioned that in other similar executions in the areas occupied by the 6th Army, *Wehrmacht* soldiers had also taken part as riflemen and did so when requested by the SS-riflemen or their leaders. All of this information was then passed on to the Commander-in-Chief of the Army, Field Marshal von Reichenau."

Operational Situation Report, USSR Number 58, 8/20/1941

"The organization of both the hanging of the two Jewish murderers and the shooting can be characterized as exemplary . . . The relationship with the *Wehrmacht* remains untroubled; above all, there is a constantly growing interest in *Wehrmacht* circles in the tasks and concerns of security police work. This was especially evident during the executions. Furthermore, the *Wehrmacht* is itself engaged in promoting the accomplishment of security police tasks. Currently for example, ongoing *Wehrmacht* reports about Communist functionaries and Jews who have been identified are arriving at all offices of the *Einsatzgruppe*."

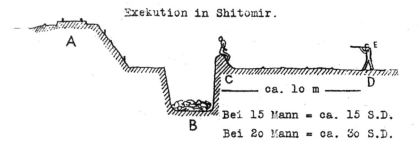

C. DIE MASSENHINRICHTUNG IN SHITOMIR.
======================================

Nachdem gefangene Ukrainer Gräben von ca. 2 m Länge, etwa 3 m Breite und etwa 3 m Tiefe ausgehoben hatten, wurden die Exekutionen gemäss Skizze durchgeführt.

Exekution in Shitomir.

Bei 15 Mann = ca. 15 S.D.
Bei 2o Mann = ca. 3o S.D.

A. = Bahndamm als Kugelfänger.

B. = Graben.

C. = Die Opfer (nicht gefesselt, Augen nicht verbunden, in Gruppen zu 15 - 2o Personen) mussten knien, Blickrichtung Damm.

C - D = Distanz: ca. 1o m.

E = SD Exekutionskommando, 1 Kdt., 2 Of. und 15 bis 3o Mann (junge Leute).

Die Leichen fielen nach vorwärts in die Grube hinein.

Der E. wollte die Sache photographieren, die Filme wurden aber noch unbelichtet durch den "Offizier" zerstört.

Bei dieser Exekution wurden ca. 5oo Personen getötet. Fluchtversuche wurden keine gemacht. "

D. JUEDISCHE OPFER:
===================

a) In Dubno (Exekution durch den E. beigewohnt)                      ca. 12o Personen.

b) In Poltawa (teilweise beigewohnt) ca. 5oo Personen.

c) In Shitomir                        ca. 5oo Personen
(Tötung von ca. 5oo Menschen durch E. gesehen. Rest der Vorgänge nicht beigewohnt.)

The mass execution in Zhytomyr: A German soldier who had witnessed the massacre in Zhytomyr fled to Switzerland towards the end of the war. He reported to authorities there on this mass shooting. This schematic depiction is attached to the transcript of his report.

1–2: At the market place in Zhytomyr, August 7, 1941.

2

## An Organized Division of Labor

The General Staff of the 6th Army was informed about and approved of the murder of Jews by the SD in the Army's territory. It took offense only when Army soldiers witnessed and photographed the executions or volunteered to take part in the murders.

In order to avoid a "growing unruliness" of the forces, von Reichenau stipulated that cooperation should occur in keeping with military regulations and orders. When requested by the SD, commanders of military administration headquarters were to provide support with their Military Police, Secret Field Police, and the Ukrainian auxiliary police. Prerequisite for the participation of soldiers was the order of a superior.

The division of labor between the *Wehrmacht* and the SS began to take shape:

• army personnel served to cordon off areas;

• Secret Field Police and Military Police participated in the arrest and guarding of Jewish civilians and delivered them to the SD;

• personnel of military administration headquarters shot "Jewish saboteurs" – the SD *Sonderkommando* annihilated the remaining men, women and children of a given place.

**Document**

Testimony of the former member of the Military Police, H. Z., *Landeskriminalamt Nordrhein-Westfalen*

"Working with the SD, who were not, however, our superiors, we Military Police had to find the Jews in their homes and make clear to them through translators that they were to assemble on the following day in a certain place at a certain time. (. . .) We had to guard the Jews until the SD came and took over. (. . .) Although we always answered the Jews' questions by telling them they would be brought to a camp – at first we ourselves didn't know otherwise – in fact, the Jews were shot outside the towns at prepared sites. In all the localities captured during the German *Wehrmacht*'s advance, the same routine was carried out. We Military Police, aided by the Russian auxiliary police who belonged to us, brought the Jews from their homes. The SD took over the Jews and led or drove them to the shooting sites."

**Document**

Testimony of the former member of the 2nd Field Telephone Communications Company/643, P. M., *Landeskriminalamt Nordrhein-Westfalen*, 7/1/1960

"Shortly after the beginning of the war in the east, my unit . . . arrived in Berdichev . . . One day, it may have been in July or August, our Sarge came looking for volunteers who would seal off the Jewish section of Berdichev. I knew what that meant, . . . word had got around, gossip had it that the Jews were to be executed. I want to emphasize that I volunteered for the barricading detail and emphasize further that no one was ordered to do it.

"I volunteered for the following reason: Not long before this I had ordered a pair of knee-high boots made by a Jew from this quarter of the city; I wanted to make sure I got my hands on them before this man was shot with the others.(. . .) I know that approximately 30 or 35 men from our company, which was made up of about 80 men at that time, volunteered for the detail. (. . .)

"At the beginning of the operation, I saw that the Ukrainian militia, interspersed with SS men and armed with clubs, was driving the Jews – men, women, children, and old people, all together – out of their houses. They went street by street. On the street the Jews were first frisked and searched for valuables. If they objected or moved slowly they were beaten to death on the spot. I personally saw hundreds of corpses lying on the streets. The Ukrainian militia was the most active in this operation, while the SS people strolled around and took charge of the delivery of valuables. The Jews were driven into an open space and were led to the site of the shooting in groups of 100 to 200 persons."

Operational Situation Report, USSR Number 80, 9/11/1941

"In Fastov, where 30 snipers and 50 Jews had already been liquidated by the Secret Field Police from post headquarters, peace could only be established after a former terrorist and the entire Jewish population between the ages of 12 and 60, a total of 262 head, had been executed by *Sonderkommando 4 a*."

Anlage 1 zum Div.Befehl Nr. 44

A b s c h r i f t !

Armeeoberkommando 6
O.Qu. / Qu. 1.

A.H.Qu., den 10.8.1941.

A n l a g e 1

Betr.: Exekutionen durch den SD.

In verschiedenen Orten des Armeegebiets werden von Organen des SD. des Reichsführers SS und Chefs der Deutschen Polizei notwendige Exekutionen an verbrecherischen, bolschewistischen, meist jüdischen Elementen durchgeführt.

Es ist vorgekommen, daß dienstfreie Soldaten sich freiwillig dem SD. zur Mithilfe bei Durchführung von Exekutionen anboten, als Zuschauer derartigen Maßnahmen beiwohnten und dabei photographische Aufnahmen machten.

Hierzu hat der Oberbefehlshaber der Armee folgendes befohlen:

Es wird jede Teilnahme von Soldaten der Armee als Zuschauer oder Ausführende bei Exekutionen, die nicht von einem militärischen Vorgesetzten befohlen sind, verboten.

Photographische Aufnahmen derartiger Exekutionen, soweit sie bisher gemacht worden sind, sind von den Disziplinarvorgesetzten einzuziehen und zu vernichten. Sie sind in Zukunft zu verbieten.

Soldaten, die gegen diesen Befehl handeln, sind wegen Disziplinlosigkeit zu bestrafen.

Tritt der SD. an Ortskommandanten mit der Bitte heran, einen für eine Exekution des SD. vorgesehenen Raum durch Absperrmannschaften gegen Zuschauer zu sichern, so ist dieser Bitte Folge zu leisten.

F. d. R. d. A.

Lt.u.Ord.Offz.

Order concerning executions by the SD: In numerous cases, *Wehrmacht* soldiers took part in mass executions of Jews by the SD as onlookers or volunteer riflemen and took photographs. Since the Commander of the 6th Army, von Reichenau, feared that the troops' morale might deteriorate as a result, he issued an order prohibiting voluntary participation in and photography at these executions.

## Belaya Tserkov'

The post headquarters in Belaya Tserkov' ordered the registration of Jews in mid-August. The Secret Field Police turned the adults over to *Sonderkommando 4a,* which had them shot by a platoon of *Waffen-SS.* Ninety children remained under guard in a building outside the city.

On August 20, two chaplains alerted the First General Staff Officer of the 295th Infantry Division, Lieutenant Colonel Groscurth, to the misery of the children, who had been locked in the house for days without food, waiting for their execution. Groscurth convinced the Commander of Military Administration Headquarters that he should postpone the murders by demanding a decision by superiors within the 6th Army.

The Commander of the 6th Army, von Reichenau, responded: "Immediately after the telephone inquiry from the Division and after consulting with *Standartenführer* Blobel (Head of the *Sonderkommando 4a*), I delayed the execution because it had not been properly arranged. I ordered that on the morning of 8/21 Blobel and the representative of the Army High Command should go to Bialacerkiev to assess the situation. As a matter of principle, I have decided that the operation, once begun, is to be carried out in a proper manner."

The Army leadership thus issued the death sentence for more than 90 children. They were executed as planned on the next day.

Report from Lieutenant Colonel Groscurth to the Chief of Staff of Army Group South on August 21, 1941

"On 8/21 at about 1100 hours, Captain Luley (Counter-intelligence Officer of AOK 6) appeared with *Standartenführer* Blobel . . . for the meeting as ordered by the Army. It took place in the office of the Commander of Military Administration Headquarters (Colonel Riedl) . . . I reported on the demands of the Division and emphasized that the Division had intervened solely because of the manner of organization. The *Standartenführer* and the *Obersturmführer* admitted to technical problems. (. . .) The Commander interjected that the initial report on the situation had come from the Division Chaplain. Captain Luley replied that although he was a Lutheran Christian, he would prefer that the pastors tend to the souls of the soldiers . . .

"As the meeting continued, the Commander of Military Administration Headquarters attempted to move the matter to the sphere of *Weltanschauung* and to bring about a discussion of fundamental questions. He explained that he considered the elimination of the Jewish women and children to be absolutely necessary, regardless of how it happened. He emphasized repeatedly that the Division's (Groscurth's) measures had unnecessarily delayed the liquidation of the children by 24 hours. The *Standartenführer* agreed . . . The *Standartenführer* explained during the discussion of further measures that the Commander-in-Chief recognized the necessity of doing away with the children and wished for it to be done, now that, in the present case, the measures had been initiated. The fact that this was indeed the position of the Commander-in-Chief had already been verified by the Intelligence Officer of AOK 6.

"Next the details of the shootings to be carried out were determined. They are to take place before the evening of 8/22. I did not take part in the details of this discussion. . . During the negotiations, the impression arose that all of the executions are the result of a proposal by the Commander of Military Administration Headquarters. The execution of all of the Jews of the city led necessarily to the liquidation of the Jewish children, especially the infants. . . . The Commander of Military Administration Headquarters and the Lieutenant declared that it was impossible to find other quarters for the children, whereby the Commander declared several times that this spawn must be exterminated. Groscurth"

1: View of the city of Belaya Tserkov', Summer 1941.

2–4: From the wallet of a soldier, handwritten note on the back: "Entry into Belaya Tserkov', 8/3/1941."

3: "Quarters in Belaya Tserkov'."

4: "Roll call in Belaya Tserkov'"

## Kiev – Babi Yar

The cooperation between *SS-Kommandos* and the 6th Army was now well established: After localities with a sizeable Jewish population had been taken over, the local *Wehrmacht* commanders made arrangements with the *SD Einsatzkommandos*. The local commanders called on Jews to assemble, bringing their valuables with them. Propaganda Company 637 printed the posters. SS and police forces escorted the victims, who thought they were to be relocated, to the murder sites on the outskirts of the town or village. They were shot there by members of the *Sonderkommando* or members of the *Waffen-SS*.

On September 27, 1941, the Commander of Military Administration Headquarters in Kiev held a meeting. Counter-intelligence officers, engineering officers, members of the SD, the police and the Secret Field Police were present. Although the "evacuation of the Jews" was discussed, those present knew that they were talking about murder. The SS shot, by their own accounts, 33,771 Jews in the Babi Yar ravine on September 29 and 30. Afterwards, an engineering unit dynamited the edges of the ravine and covered the mass grave.

**Document**

Summons by the Commander of the Military Administration Headquarters, Kiev

"All Jews from the city of Kiev and surroundings are to gather on Monday September 29, 1941 by 8 o'clock at the corner of Melnik and Dokterivski Streets (at the cemeteries). Documents, money and valuables, as well as warm clothing, underclothes etc., are to be brought along. Anyone who does not obey this order and is found elsewhere will be shot. Anyone who enters dwellings left by Jews or takes objects from them will be shot."

**Document**

Operational Situation Report, USSR Number 128, 11/3/1941

"The difficulties arising from carrying out such a large operation – above all in getting the Jews to gather – were overcome in Kiev by plastering the walls with posters ordering the Jewish population to relocate. Although expectations were that 5,000 to 6,000 Jews would take part, over 30,000 Jews appeared who, as a result of extremely skillful organization, still believed they were going to be relocated immediately before their execution."

**Document**

Letter from the field, Private Ludwig B., 296th Infantry Division, from Kiev, 9/28/1941

"We are no longer in action. I don't think that we will see further action. But even so it is dangerous everywhere because of the many mines still set. In Kiev, for example, there is one explosion after another due to mines. The city has been burning for eight days, everything is done by the Jews. In response the Jews from the ages of 14 to 60 have been shot and the wives of the Jews will be shot too, otherwise there will be no end to this . . ."

1–2: Victims on the road to Babi Yar.

2

4–5: Covering the mass grave.

3–8: The murder sites

5

6–7: Uniformed men go through the belongings of the murder victims.

7

8

## The Reichenau order

On October 10, 1941, von Reichenau issued an order that Hitler praised and immediately distributed throughout the entire *Wehrmacht* as exemplary.

"RE: Conduct of the troops in the East. In many instances, confusion still prevails regarding the conduct of the troops in their dealings with the Bolshevist system. The primary goal of the campaign against the Jewish-Bolshevist system is the absolute destruction of the means of power and the eradication of Asian influence in the European cultural sphere. As a result, tasks arise for the troops that transcend traditional one-dimensional soldiership.

"The soldier in the East is not only a fighter according to the rules of the art of waging war, but also the bearer of the inexorable *völkische* concept and the avenger of all the bestialities that were visited on the Germans and related peoples [*artverwandtem Volkstum*]. Therefore the soldier must fully understand the necessity for severe but just atonement by the Jewish subhumanity [*Untermenschentum*]. This has the further goal of nipping in the bud uprisings to the rear of the *Wehrmacht* which, as experience shows, are always instigated by Jews . . .

"The soldier has two tasks to fulfill, far removed from all political considerations about the future:

1) the utter destruction of Bolshevist heresy, of the Soviet state and its war machine,

2) the merciless extermination of foreign [*artfremder*] cunning and cruelty, thereby securing the life of the German *Wehrmacht* in Russia. This is the only way we can live up to our historic task of liberating the German people once and for all from the Asiatic-Jewish peril.

Commander-in-Chief von Reichenau
Field Marshal."

Walter von Reichenau: A biography

| | |
|---|---|
| Born: | October 18, 1884 in Karlsruhe |
| 1903: | Officer Candidate with the 1st Regiment of the Field Artillery Guards |
| 1904: | Second Lieutenant |
| 1912: | First Lieutenant |
| 1914: | Captain with the 1st Regiment of the Reserve Field Artillery Guards |
| 1915: | 47th Reserve Division |
| 1916: | Rear Area Inspection (General Staff) in Woyrsch |
| 1917: | 87th Infantry Division<br>3rd Reserve Division (General Staff) |
| 1918: | 11th Infantry Division (General Staff) |
| 1919: | 7th Cavalry Rifle Division (General Staff) |
| 1923–1926: | General Staff of the 3rd Division |
| 1924: | Major |
| 1927: | Staff Army Group Headquarters. 1 |
| 1929: | Lieutenant Colonel |
| 1929–1931: | Chief of Staff of the 1st Division |
| 1932: | Colonel |
| 1933: | Head of the Minister's Office in the Reich Army Ministry |
| 1934: | Brigadier General, Head of the *Wehrmacht* Office |
| 1935: | Major General; Commanding General of the VIIth Army Corps |
| 1936: | General of the Artillery |
| 1939: | Commander-in-Chief of the 10th Army, Senior General |
| 1940: | Commander-in-Chief of the 6th Army, Field Marshal |
| Died: | January 17, 1942 in a plane crash while being flown from Poltawa to Germany following a stroke |

This order was not a spontaneous impulse on the part of Field Marshal Reichenau, but the summation of what his 6th Army had been practicing since June 22, 1941.

A few days later, the Commander of Lubny, a town east of Kiev, had the Jewish population come to a gathering place "for relocation." There the *Sonderkommando 4a* took charge of the 1,800 Jews and shot them.

Walter von Reichenau, left.

Lubny, October 16, 1941: The Jewish population before being shot

By mid-July 1941, the General Staff of the 6th Army had institutionalized the increasingly ruthless treatment of civilians in the occupied territories. The methods of persecution which individual units had begun to practice became the norm for all units under its command.

In a Command Directive issued on July 10, the High Command of the 6th Army (AOK 6) stipulated – under the pretext of security – that the following measures were to be taken after localities were captured:

"a) Soldiers in civilian dress, usually recognizable by their short hair, are to be shot as soon as it has been determined that they are Red soldiers. (Exception – deserters!)

b) Civilians who are hostile in posture or action, especially those who support the Red Army (for example, by facilitating communication with Red troops living in the forests), are to be executed as irregulars.

c) Unreliable elements, for example Soviet civil functionaries in localities . . . are to be arrested immediately. When troops depart, such arrested elements are to be turned over, when possible, to the Military Police or to the SD *Einsatzkommando*" (Command Directive of the AOK 6, July 10, 1941)

In a further Command Directive dated July 19, the AOK 6 ordered "collective measures" when, after acts of sabotage, the saboteurs could not be determined. Jews or Russians were to be shot and their houses burned down.

Political commissars were not the only targets of the 6th Army's selective manhunts among the Red Army POWs. In late July 1941, Army officials notified their prison camps to deal with political intolerables and "suspicious elements" "according to previously issued special orders." Jewish prisoners of war were turned over to the SD.

By agreement with the High Command of the Army (OKH), the AOK 6 left it up to troop commanders to declare that Red Army soldiers were partisans as they saw fit and to shoot them on the spot. Some divisions went even farther: the 75th Infantry Division shot women in uniform – *"Flintenweiber"* or gun women in *Wehrmacht* parlance – and other prisoners in reprisal for German soldiers killed in battle.

1-7: Combing a village for "partisans." (Photos by the Propaganda Companies.)

2

3

98

4

5

6

7

8: Arrest of "soldiers in civilian clothes"

99

**Document**

Operational Situation Report, USSR Number 132, 11/12/1941

"Included in the total of those executed by the *Sonderkommando 4 a* . . . in the second half of the month of October are again, along with a relatively small number of political functionaries, active Communists, saboteurs, etc., primarily Jews, and a large part of these are Jewish prisoners of war turned over by the *Wehrmacht*. Following a request by the commanding officer of the local POW camp in Borispol, 742 Jewish prisoners of war were shot by a platoon of *Sonderkommando 4 a* on 10/14/41 and 357 on 10/16/41, including several commissars and 78 wounded Jewish POWs turned over by the camp doctor."

**Document**

Report by Colonel Erwin Lahousen, Foreign Intelligence Office of the OKW, on 10/23/1941, entitled "Observations and findings while travelling in the East"

"The columns of Russian prisoners of war moving on the roads make an idiotic impression like herds of animals. The guard details, made up in part of non-military units as for example members of the Reich Labor Service and small in comparison to the number of prisoners, can only maintain some semblance of order . . . by using physical force. Because of the physical exertion of the marches, the meager diet and poor conditions in the quarters in individual camps, prisoners of war often break down, are then carried by their fellow-soldiers or are left lying. The 6th Army has given orders that all prisoners of war who break down are to be executed. Unfortunately, this is done on the road, even in towns . . ."

1–8: Photos by the Propaganda Companies with original captions.

2

100

3: "Everywhere they are forced out of their burrows, disarmed and taken prisoner, . . .

4

5: . . . and then the men of the advance detachment enter the village . . .

6

7: . . . Among the numerous dead . . . a *Flintenweib* as well."

8: "Soviet *Flintenweib* killed by German anti-tank fire." (Photo suppressed by the censor.)

# Looting the Ukraine

During preparations for "Operation Barbarossa," the attack on the Soviet Union, the High Command of the Armed Forces and the Reich Ministry for Food and Agriculture had agreed to ruthlessly exploit the occupied territories to improve the food supply in Germany. To ease the pressure on the supply lines to the East, the *Wehrmacht* was to procure its own foodstuffs in the occupied territories. From the beginning, then, the starvation of millions of people was part of the plan.

According to calculations of the Reich Ministry for Food and Agriculture, the Soviet Union's grain surplus amounted to 8.7 million tons, 600,000 tons of which were to be transported to Germany. Especially the Ukrainian "bread basket" was to supply huge amounts of foodstuffs.

Because it was considered a foregone conclusion that the Soviet Union would be conquered in the course of a few weeks, the Eastern Army had begun "Operation Barbarossa" with only 20 days' rations. Experts did not, however, calculate that the *Wehrmacht* would soon be able to procure all necessary provisions in the Soviet Union or that the food shortages in Germany would be eased within a short time. In any case, they expected harvest surpluses only in the southern Ukraine.

Armee-Oberkommando 6
— Abt. III — Az. 14 n —

*KTB*

A. H. Qu., den 31. Juli 1941

## Armeebefehl!

Das eigenmaechtige Beutemachen ist verboten. Kriegsbeute gehoert dem Staat, nicht dem Einzelnen. Aneignen von Privateigentum ist Pluenderung, die in schweren Faellen mit dem Tode zu bestrafen ist. Selbstaendiges Herumsuchen in Haeusern ist verboten.

Beitreibungen fuer die Beduerfnisse der Truppe duerfen nur auf Befehl eines Offiziers oder Beamten im Offiziersrange erfolgen, der einem Beitreibungskommando stets ausser einem Ausweis auch den erforderlichen Requisitionsschein (Quittung) auszustellen hat.

Ich erwarte von allen Vorgesetzten, dass sie mit der gebotenen Strenge die Mannszucht als Grundlage des Sieges aufrechterhalten und diesen Befehlen Geltung verschaffen.

Der Oberbefehlshaber:

**v. Reichenau**

Generalfeldmarschall.

Verteilt
bis Kpn., Bttrn. usw.

Army orders: To counteract the increase in looting by the troops, Reichenau issued an order on July 31, 1941 which was aimed at enforcing general rules for procuring provisions and imposed severe penalties for unauthorized plundering. In practice, this order had only a minor effect, in particular since the supply situation began to deteriorate drastically in the fall of 1941.

1–8: Photos by the Propaganda Companies.

2–3: Grain harvest under supervision of the *Wehrmacht*.

3

4: "Grain for the benefit of the victor."

5

6

7

8: Delivery of grain from the Ukraine to Berlin.

## "Living off the land"

It quickly became evident that the goal of satisfying the needs of the entire *Wehrmacht* solely with foodstuffs from the Soviet Union as early as 1941 was unrealistic. In early July 1941, the General Quartermaster of the 6th Army ordered that every opportunity to acquire food and clothing be exploited. The dividing lines between requisitioning under orders and free-lance looting grew less and less clear.

At the end of September, the delivery of supplies to the troops was again reduced. The Army High Command 6 gave instructions to lay in stocks of food for the winter. Because the Red Army had taken or destroyed the available provisions, units of the 6th Army fought over the meager remains. Collecting foodstuffs took on forms that led von Reichenau to issue the aforementioned order, aimed at securing discipline during requisitioning. But the order failed to prevent wild looting. Troop commanders were forced to allow looting in their own interest, in order to forestall impending food shortages.

---

Documents

From the War Journal of the General Quartermaster of the 6th Army: "Special instructions on supplies"

**"7/3/41**

In view of the difficult transportation situation and considering the food situation in the homeland, foodstuffs can be supplied only to the extent that is absolutely necessary.

It is thus of primary importance that the troops, whenever possible, live off the land. Every opportunity should be exploited."

**"7/15/41**

Some units have undertaken 'illicit requisitions,' i.e. taking livestock, food, etc. from the rural Ukrainian population without issuing a requisition receipt. Political concerns require that these sorts of theft from the Ukrainian population must be stopped, regardless of the circumstances. Units under this command are to be informed immediately on this account."

**"7/16/41**

Because further supplies of the most necessary clothing and maintenance material cannot be expected for some time and because the homeland must be spared by all means from pressures on raw materials, all available spoils of war are to be registered and used. This pertains, above all, to boots and shoes. Shoes and boots are to be taken from dead Russian soldiers and prisoners of war and used at least for repairs and replacement soles. As an emergency measure, available shoes and boots and materials suitable for foot coverings are to be purchased from the civilian population without consideration of their nationality. Forced purchases are also permissible. In cases where looting of clothing stores by the population becomes known, the local commander is to set a time limit for the return of the clothing, under the threat of execution."

---

Document

Report from Colonel Erwin Lahousen, Foreign Intelligence Office of the OKW
10/23/1941

"The population welcomes German soldiers as liberators from the Bolshevist yoke. Nonetheless, there is danger that these sentiments, which are extremely favorable for us and are manifested in extraordinary hospitality and gifts, will reverse themselves as the result of bad treatment. The opinion has been expressed in various German agencies and units that it is time to put a stop to German sentimentality and to use force against Ukrainians who object to the removal of furniture, paintings, and the like. This practice has already degenerated to a kind of looting, justified by the argument that this is, in effect, not private property but property of the Russian State."

"Warning": Although plundering was subject to the death penalty, in the winter of 1941/42, the commanders of the Sixth Army were forced to constantly repeat their warnings against it.

1–6: "Living off the land."

2

3

4

5

6

The battle against "vagabonds"

The 6th Army's offensive bogged down in early November 1941 in the Kharkov region. Following looting by the divisions, scarcely anything was left for the native population. The food situation was especially catastrophic in the cities. Tens of thousands of Ukrainians crisscrossed the country, looking for food and fuel. Thousands of them fell victim to the anti-partisan units organized by the 6th Army in the interim.

Suspicious persons, men and women both, were tortured and shot. Houses and entire villages were burned to the ground because individual inhabitants had supposedly supported partisans. Hostages were shot and "accomplices" were hanged.

With its brutal repression of civilians along the front, the 6th Army created the enemies it supposedly was fighting. From mid-December 1941 on, villages were evacuated and burned to the ground for tactical reasons. The inhabitants were deported and those who returned to their villages were shot.

**Document**

Order of the Town Commander's Office I/927, 11/18/1941

"1.) All male civilians who wander around and cannot identify themselves are to be arrested and turned over to the Secret Field Police in Sumy.

2.) The following are valid as identification:
a) identification papers from the Town Commander's Office,
b) POW certificates of discharge,
c) identification papers from the city administration, in so far as they are authorized by the Town Commander's Office.

3.) Civilians of both sexes found loitering between 1800 hours and 500 hours are to be arrested and when resisting arrest are to be shot immediately.

4.) Civilians who are found with weapons and ammunition of any sort and who do not possess identification papers from German military authorites are to be shot immediately."

**Document**

War Journal AOK 6, Intelligence Section, 12/7/1941

"The Army reports to the Army Group that in the region occupied by the Army the partisan movement is as good as defeated. It attributes this to the strict measures that were employed. Along with the actual partisans, many elements straying around the countryside without identification, who are in fact the agents and communications service of the partisans, were also done away with. In the course of this operation in the region occupied by the Army, several thousand were publicly hanged and shot. Experience shows that death by hanging is an especially effective deterrent. In Kharkov, several hundred partisans and suspicious elements were hanged in the city. Since then acts of sabotage have ceased. One can establish from experience: Only measures which the population fears more than partisan acts of terror will lead us to our goal."

**Document**

War Journal of the 75th Infantry Division, Intelligence Section, 12/23/1941

"As ordered, villages are being burned to the ground on the front lines and immediately behind them. These operations are being pursued with all means."

War Journal of the 75th Infantry Divison Intelligence Section, January 1942

"As of today the male civilian population is forbidden to leave towns and villages for any reason. The troops are to make this known to mayors. Every male civilian found outside the limits of a town or village is to be shot. Civilians who are in the service of the *Wehrmacht* are to be given impeccable identification papers and a white armband."

"In Massoyedvo, 15 civilians found roaming around were shot."

"In Massoyedvo, 12 civilians found loitering were shot."

1: In front of post headquarters.

2: Inspection of travelling civilians at a *Wehrmacht* checkpoint.

3–4: Photos taken by a soldier, handwritten note on the back: "In Sumy. Now you can see the partisans' chins drop!"

4

1–5: Photos taken by a soldier, handwritten note on the back: "A hanging in Bogodukhov."

2

7

6–9: Execution of villagers.

3

4

5

8

9

# Kharkov

## Gallows

The last large city taken by the 6th Army was Kharkov at the end of October 1941. The city's Jewish inhabitants as well as a substantial portion of the rest of the civilian population fell victim to the occupation politics of the *Wehrmacht* and SS. Shortly before taking the city, the Army High Command 6 ordered the Staff of the LVth Army Corps assigned to administer the city to act "with unscrupulous severity" against "enemy elements." "Jewish and Bolshevist persons" were to be selected preferentially as targets for collective "atonement." "Saboteurs" were to be hanged publicly.

When explosive charges laid by the retreating Red Army detonated in November, the Commander of Military Administration Headquarters had hundreds of civilians, mainly male Jews, arrested and hanged in the streets of Kharkov in retribution.

Documents

From the private notes of the 2nd Adjutant of the LVth Army Corps, Kharkov, 11/28/1941

"November 14, 1941: Tonight there was a muffled bang: Although the "Red Army" building had been searched with all the tricks of the trade, it exploded tonight with the staff of the 60th Division inside; the Division Commander, the Chief of Staff, the First General Staff Officer and 4 clerks were found dead and horribly mangled. During the day 4 other buildings exploded . . . 200 Communists were shot or hanged and 1,000 hostages taken in retribution.

"November 28, 1941: The concentration camp has been reduced to 400 head, among them 300 Jews."

Document

Meeting at the Kharkov Headquarters on 11/4/1941: War Journal, 57th Infantry Division Second General Staff Officer

"Cleansing operations [are] still underway, but work has become very difficult because as opposed to other places, no materials and no lists were found in Kharkov. Individual informers have been called in, in Kharkov there are also many emigrants from all over the world. The Jews [are], in particular, who are often left behind as contacts or communications agents, are suspected. Since Jews [are] for the most part still in hiding, operation against the Jews [is] planned for sometime later. Meanwhile, the Head Rabbi of the local Jews to deliver all gold and currency for 'protection' of Jewish property."

1–3: Hangings from the balconies of Kharkov, November 1941.

2

3

1–8: Hangings from the balconies of Kharkov, November 1941.

2

3

4

5

6

7

8

## Hunger

In response to the desperate food and supply situation in Kharkov, the Quartermaster Section of the 6th Army suggested the evacuation of the entire civilian population.

The counter-intelligence officer, however, advocated a program of selective mass murder, calling for the "registration of all Jews, political commissars and of the politically suspicious, and of all who are not local residents." He suggested leaving their arrest and murder to the SD. The Military Administration Headquarters left the problem of procuring foodstuffs entirely in the hands of the Ukrainian civilian authorities. Because there were no public stockpiles, they were to requisition private supplies and divide them equally.

In December 1941, the first deaths by starvation occurred and by January 1942 a third of the 300,000 inhabitants were suffering from malnutrition. Because forced evacuation and deportation of the civilian population to the East was considered an unreasonable task for the troops, the city headquarters facilitated voluntary emigration by handing out travel permits. The population, however, used these primarily for trips to the countryside to procure food. In doing so, they ran the risk of being shot as "vagabonds."

Document

From the private notes of the 2nd Adjutant of the LVth Army Corps, Kharkov, 11/13/ and 12/6/1941

"11/13/1941:

In IIb [Personnel Office for Enlisted Men] the first reports are going around about incidents involving the troops: A Jew was 'separated' from his fur coat; while the Russian mayor was in the 'office,' soldiers emptied out his apartment; a Russian woman was locked in a cellar and raped by 6! soldiers, one after the other."

"12/6/1941:

We turned over the city's Military Administration Headquarters to the 57th Infantry Division. That will save us a lot of work. There were loads of reports coming in each day: Looting of the civilian population by soldiers, removal of food supplies, illegal 'confiscation' of objects, rape of women. [. . .] The Commanding General orders that these incidents are not to be subject to prosecution, but rather to be dealt with as disciplinary cases by the Second General Staff Officer."

Document

Commander of the Army Group South Rear Area , Department VII, Report 12/1–12/15/1941

"On 12/2, there was a meeting with representatives from the military administration groups of the Security Division and representatives of a number of local military administration headquarters. It was stated that the most pressing problem is feeding the population . . . The food situation in Kharkov (about 600,000 inhabitants) is so bad that there are daily deaths from starvation. It has not been possible up to now to bring even close to sufficient amounts of food into the city, due to insufficient transportation and because there are no stockpiles of food in the vicinity."

## Murder of Jews

In the first half of December 1941, *Sonderkommando 4 a*, after consulting with army leadership and Military Administration Headquarters, disseminated a summons to all Jewish men, women and children to gather for relocation. More than 20,000 persons who answered the summons were driven out of the city and brought to a tractor factory that the 6th Army had requisitioned. Before the end of the year, the *Sonderkommando 4 a* had shot some of them. Starting in January 1942, it murdered the rest of them in a truck equipped for gassing.

Document

Operational Situation Report, USSR Number 164, 2/4/1942

"The foremost concern was finding a suitable site for the evacuation of the Jews, in closest cooperation with the housing office of the city. A site was chosen where the Jews could be housed in workers' barracks on the grounds of a factory settlement. On 12/14/41, a summons from the City Commander to the Jews of Kharkov was issued in which they were required to go to the settlement described therein by 12/16/41. The evacuation of the Jews proceeded smoothly except for several looting incidents that took place during the march of the Jews to the new quarters, incidents involving almost exclusively Ukrainians. To date, there is no exact figure on the number of Jews included in the evacuation. Counting of the Jews has begun. Simultaneously, preparations for shooting the Jews are in progress. 305 of the Jews who had spread rumors detrimental to the German *Wehrmacht* were shot immediately."

1

2: Poster written in Ukrainian with the headline: "The Jew – Your eternal enemy" and the last two lines: "Stalin and the Jews – A gang of criminals."

Hannes Heer Russia: Three Years of Occupation, 1941–1944

When German *Wehrmacht* formations crossed into the Soviet Union on June 22, 1941 without a declaration of war, they formed three spearheads designed to annihilate the majority of the Soviet armed forces and to penetrate deep into the interior of the country.

By July 23, 1941, the Army Group Center had occupied White Russia with its capital city Minsk and advanced as far as Smolensk.

In a second offensive, which began in October, large sections of central Russia were occupied, before the advance finally came to a halt outside of Moscow on December 5, 1941.

The western part of White Russia was governed by a civilian administration, while the eastern half remained under military administration. Of all the Soviet republics, White Russia experienced the longest period of German occupation.

This case study illustrates more clearly than any other the aims and the outcomes of Nazi occupation: 2.2 million of a total of 10.6 million residents of White Russia before the occupation, lost their lives.

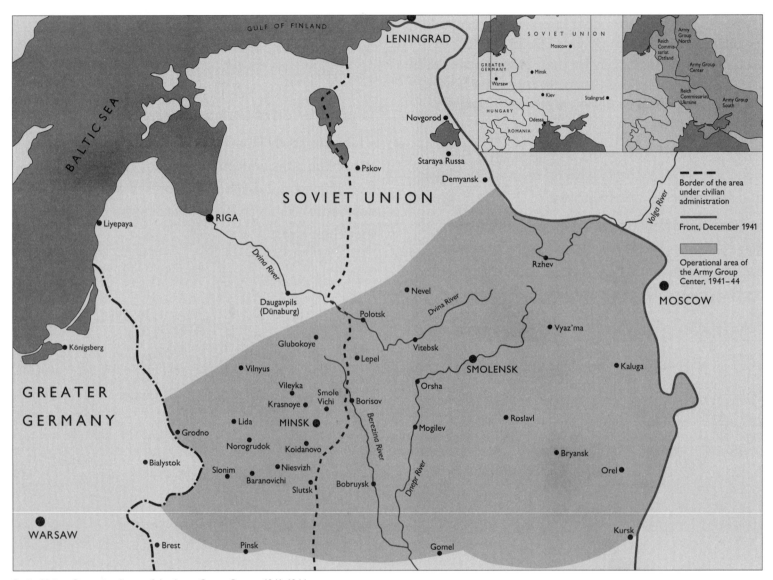

Soviet Union: Operational area of the Army Group Center, 1941–1944.

Minsk: A case study

German bombers turned Minsk into a pile of ruins. When tank [Panzer] spearheads of the Army Group Center reached the city on June 28, 100,000 of the approximately 250,000 inhabitants fell into German hands; half of these were Jews. All inhabitants were required to report to local Military Administration Headquarters for registration and had to obey strict occupation laws and regulations. From the very beginning, however, the Jews were subject to much harsher treatment.

• In the first, undated, order issued by the commander for the occupied territories, the Jews were ordered to register and to wear a yellow star; people were forbidden to greet Jews.

• Order Number 2, dated July 13, rescinded the right of Jews to change their places of residence and jobs and ordered that they be "pooled" in Jewish sections of the city; the Jewish communities were forced to establish Jewish councils [*Judenräte*] to oversee the implementation of Nazi Orders.

• On July 19, the Commander of the Military Administration in Minsk specified the order of his superior: Within five days all Jews had to be "resettled" in the ghetto, with permission to leave only when they were led out under guard to do forced labor.

These measures degraded the Jews to a anonymous mass deprived of its rights and destined for systematic annihilation. The first victims were the members of the Jewish intelligentsia. On July 22, 1941 the *Wehrmacht's* economic administration in occupied White Russia summarized with satisfaction the results of a month of occupation:

"Jews suspected of agitation have been shot in large numbers amounting to several thousand persons. As a result, the Jewish population is intimidated and eager to work."

(Economic Inspection of the Army Group Center, Situation Report, July 22, 1941)

1–3: Occupation of the city of Minsk, June 1941.

2

3

Minsk, July 19, 1941
Order

1. As of the date of this order, a Jewish residential area is established in Minsk that is to be inhabited exclusively by Jews.

2. The entire Jewish population of the city of Minsk must immediately relocate into the Jewish residential area of the city of Minsk within 5 times 24 hours after publication of this order. Anyone who is found outside the area indicated after this deadline will be arrested and severely punished.

3. Relocation with furnishings and household items is permitted. Bringing the property of others will be punished with the death penalty.

4. The residential area is bordered by the following streets: Kolkhosniy Piereulok, junction: Kolkhosnaya Street, junction along the river, junction: Nemigskaya Street, excepting the Orthodox Church, junction: Respublikanska Street, junction: Shornaya Street, junction: Kolektornaya Street, junction: Mebelney Piereulok, junction: Perekopskaya Street, junction Nisovaya Street, junction: Jewish Cemetery wall, junction: Saslavskaya, junction: to the corner of Kolkhesniy Piereulok.

5. After relocation has been concluded, the Jewish residential area is to be isolated from the rest of the city by walls. Inhabitants of the Jewish residential area are to construct the walls with the available bricks from uninhabitable houses.

6. Jews who are members of labor crews are not permitted to stay outside their assigned residential area. They may leave the residential area in labor crews only and are permitted to remain outside the area only while doing work assigned by the city administration of Minsk. Violations will be punished with the death penalty.

7. Jews are permitted to enter and leave the Jewish residential area through the 2 entrances on Opanski and Ostrovski Streets only. Crossing the perimeter walls is forbidden. German guards and auxiliary police have orders to shoot violators.

8. With the exception of members of German units and the Minsk Municipal Administration on official business, only Jews may enter the Jewish residential area.

9. The *Judenrat* must pay 30,000 *Tscherwonzen* as a compulsory loan to finance administrative measures associated with relocation. This sum is to be paid to the Cashier's Office of the Municipal Administration, Karl Marks [sic] Street 28, within 12 hours after publication of this order; interest rates will be settled at a later date.

10. Immediately after relocation, the *Judenrat* must inform the Housing Office of the Municipal Administration about dwellings outside of the Jewish residential area which have been vacated by Jews and have not yet been occupied by members of the Aryan population.

11. Order in the Jewish residential area will be maintained by a Jewish office for that purpose. (Special instructions to follow.)

12. The *Judenrat* of the city of Minsk is fully responsible for the thorough execution of Jewish relocation. Violations will be severely punished.
Commander of Military Administration Headquarters

1: Map of the Minsk ghetto.

2: The Minsk ghetto.

3–4: "Relocation" into the Minsk ghetto.

4

1–3: "Relocation" into the Minsk ghetto.

2

3

4–8: Establishment of ghettos elsewhere in White
Russia.
4–6: Mogilev.

6

5

7–8: Grodno.

8

## Forced laborers serving the *Wehrmacht*

The ghettos had been placed under the authority of the respective local military administration headquarters of the *Wehrmacht*. White Russia was of special strategic importance for the Army Group Center, since corridors for key supply lines and crucial armament factories and repair facilities were located within its borders. The hundreds of thousands of Jews imprisoned in ghettos were used as work slaves in the army's rear area.

The civilian administration established in September 1941 to govern the western part of White Russia also assumed responsibility for the economic exploitation of the ghettos. Politically, the civilian administration was placed under the authority of Himmler's Security Service (SD); but the Army was still the main beneficiary of the "*Arbeitsjuden*" [work Jews] and was responsible for their "annihilation through work." In eastern White Russia, in the rear area of Army Group Center, the *Wehrmacht* remained in command of the ghettos.

Excerpts from the memoirs of Heinz Rosenberg, a German Jew who survived the Minsk ghetto: "Jahre des Schreckens" ("Years of Terror"), Göttingen 1992.

"A commando of 100 men was working in an army camp sorting Russian rifles and other material. One day the sergeant on duty found a rifle in the bushes and had all the men locked in a barracks and ordered them to name the one who had hidden the rifle within two hours.

"When the two hours were up, no one stepped forward to be punished for a crime he hadn't committed. The SS commander was then summoned. A group of men from the SS Security Service appeared, stood the 100 Jewish workers in a row, selected ten of them and shot them on the spot. Among them was Gabi's father, a lawyer who had been an officer in the First World War. He was heroic enough to shout at the SS men: 'You swine! I was good enough to fight for Germany in the First World War. I received medals, I have a wife and child. And you shoot me for nothing. I spit on you!' The 90 survivors then had to carry the corpses to a mass grave."

1–2: Forced laborers working on the railroad in Minsk, February 1942.

2

3: Labor card of a Jewish woman in Minsk, 1943.

4–7: Forced labor in the service of the *Wehrmacht* in Mogilev, photos by the Propaganda Companies, 1941.

5

6

7

8: Forced laborers in Minsk, 1942

# "The cleansing of the countryside"

Images of the enemy

From the beginning, the High Command of the *Wehrmacht* aimed to expose Jews as especially dangerous enemies. In the "Guidelines for the Conduct of the Troops in Russia," (May 19, 1941), Bolshevism was identified as "the mortal enemy" of the German people. The battle against this mortal enemy demanded "ruthless measures against Bolshevist agitators, irregulars, saboteurs, Jews."

The message was spelled out quite simply for the *Landser*, the common soldier: Every Jew is a partisan or a supporter of the partisans.

Responsibility for propagating this image of the enemy was in the hands of the Propaganda Companies and the counter-intelligence officers.

`Document`

221st Security Division, War Journal, 7/8/1941

"Wherever Jews live, cleansing the area [becomes] difficult . . . since the Jews support the creation of partisan groups and the perpetration of local disturbances by stragglers from the Russian Army."

`Document`

Infantry Regiment 350, Report of the Battalion Commander, 8/18/1941

"Finally, it is of utmost importance that we eradicate the influence of the Jews and eliminate these elements by the most radical means, since they are precisely the ones . . . who maintain connections with the Red Army and with the bandits whom we are fighting."

`Document`

403rd Security Division, Activity Report, Intelligence Section
August 1941

"In lectures to the company, the Staff Intelligence Officer is pointing out the danger and despicableness of having anything to do with Jews or Jewesses. There is repeated confirmation of the good-naturedness and forgetfulness of the German people in general, whose chivalrous behavior when dealing with defenseless persons also carries over to this race."

`Document`

SS Cavalry Brigade, Activity Report dated 9/3/1941, for the period 8/25–9/3/1941

"Contacts between partisan detachments are maintained primarily by Jews."

`Document`

*Wehrmacht* Commander *Ostland* / Commandant White Ruthenia, Situation Report, dated 9/10/1941, for the period 9/1–9/10/1941

"The Jewish class, which makes up the largest part of the population in the cities, is the driving force behind the resistance movement emerging in various places."

1: Propaganda poster: "Under the Jewish banner."

2–3: Photos by the Propaganda Companies with original captions. "Not even worth a bullet: These animalized Jews betrayed 5 German solders to the Reds; the men betrayed were taken prisoner and tortured to death by Red Army soldiers. The Jews shown here were executed immediately. Date: June, 28, 1941."

3: "Soviet Russian prisoners. To the right a rabbi who is not a soldier but a bandit leader and instigator of countless acts of terror. Date: August 1941."

## Hunting Jews

Propaganda was not the end of the story. The *Wehrmacht* commander of the General Commissariat White Ruthenia ordered his units "to make sure that the Jews are completely eliminated from the villages." According to his account, Jews were the sole supporters of the partisan movement. "Therefore, their annihilation is to be pursued ruthlessly."

> (The Commandant in White Ruthenia, October 16, 1941)

Former members of Infantry Regiment 727 assigned to such duty described what took place. The soldiers surrounded the villages and farms, drove the Jews together and executed them next to ditches dug for this purpose. The villages in the rear area of Army Group Center were "cleansed" of Jews in the same manner.

`Document`

Interrogation of former Private G. of the 6th Company, Infantry Regiment 727, on 9/26/1962

"The Company undertook minor operations in the vicinity of Slonim. We were transported in trucks, sometimes we marched . . . During one of these operations I had to escort the truck taking approximately 20 Jews to a pit . . . The truck driver transported many Jews to the execution site. I believe that 100 Jews were shot on this day . . . I know that we also collected Jews once in front of the schoolhouse and shot them. This was about 100 Jews. When we drove Jews from the houses on such occasions, we always had instructions from the town commander G. to make the Jews think that they were going to be brought to collecting point camps or to internment camps and that they should take their belongings with them."

`Document`

Interrogation of L., former clerk with the 12th Company of Infantry Regiment 727, on 12/9/1964

"Lieutenant S. repeatedly went on patrols . . . On these so-called patrols S. drove around the area with his men. When he returned he reported to the head clerk of the company that numerous partisans had been shot during the operation. It was generally known in the company that it was really Jews he was talking about."

`Document`

Private Richard Heidenreich, 12th Company of Infantry Regiment 254, Journal Entry 10/5/1941

"There were approximately 1,000 Jews in the village of Krupka and all of them had to be shot today . . . At exactly 7 a. m., all Jews – men, women, and children – had to report to the inspection grounds. After roll call, the column marched to the nearest swamp. The Jews had been told that they were all to be deported to Germany to work. But many of them guessed what was in store for them, especially when we crossed the narrow-gauge railroad tracks and marched on toward the swamp. Panic broke out . . . When we arrived at the swamp, they were ordered to sit down facing the direction from which they had come. 50 meters farther was a deep ditch full of water. The first ten had to stand next to that ditch and undress to the waist. Then they had to climb down into the ditch and those of us who were to shoot them stood on the edge above them. A lieutenant and a sergeant stood next to us. There were ten shots, ten Jews were mowed down. This went on until all were finished off. Only a few of them kept their composure. The children clung to their mothers, wives to their husbands. I won't easily forget that sight. A few days later a similarly large number were executed in Kholopanichi. I took part in that as well. But there was no swamp there. There was only a ditch in the sand, in which the Jews were pickled. A couple of days later the entire regiment was transferred to Gorki by way of Orsha."

## The temporary end of the "cleansings"

"For a while, the *Wehrmacht* did a thorough job of cleansing the countryside; unfortunately, only in places with less than 1,000 inhabitants."

> (Regional Commissar Erren in Slonim, 1/25/1942)

With these words, formulated in January 1942, a representative of the civilian administration criticized the fact that the *Wehrmacht* had suddenly ceased its "Jew hunt." It had done so not out of moral scruples, but because the winter offensive of the Red Army required every man. By January 1942, the *Wehrmacht* had murdered 20,000 Jews in White Russia.

1–3: Original captions of the Landeskriminalamt Baden-Württemberg. Jews are forced to dig a mass grave and undress and are then driven into the pit. The group includes children (photo 3). Members of the local auxiliary forces (presumably Latvians) participate in the shootings. Place and time: presumably Latvia, summer 1941.

2

3

1–2: SD and *Waffen-SS* at an execution.

2

3: *Wehrmacht* soldiers after an execution.

4–5: Members of the SD and *Wehrmacht* soldiers at an execution.

5

7

6–7: Victims are driven into the forest.

# Murder in the ghettos

## The prelude to systematic mass murder

On September 25, 1941, the *Wehrmacht* Commander *Ostland*, Major General Braemer, issued "Guidelines for maintaining peace and order in the Ostland." *Ostland* was a Nazi civilian administration entity, including the Baltic countries, parts of Poland and White Russia. According to this order,

"Peace and order are threatened by:

a) partisans,

b) Communists and other radical elements,

c) Jews and those friendly to the Jews.

"Together with the *Wehrmacht* and the police, all German organizations and individuals in the occupied territories are to assist in neutralizing these elements."

The words of this order marked the beginning of systematic mass murder in the White Russian ghettos and the beginning of the *Wehrmacht*'s active participation.

The massacres began in October – with the so-called "Operation Jew-free" *[Aktion Judenfrei]*. Following orders from the *Wehrmacht* commander, Reserve Police Battalion 11 marched from Lithuania to Minsk on October 4 to receive more specific orders from the Commander of the 707th Security Division: those orders were to "clear" the ghettos in Smolovichi, Koidanovo and Slutzk. 8,200 Jews were murdered.

Document

Reserve Police Battalion 11,
Situation Report on the special operation in Minsk 10/14/1941–10/21/1941, 10/21/1941

"On 10/14/41, 2nd, 4th Co. and 2 companies of Order Police cleansed Smilovichi (approximately 35 kilometers southeast of Minsk) of Jews, Communists, and elements hostile to Germany and liquidated 1,300 head . . . On 10/15/41 and 10/16/41 the area around Logoysk (about 40 kilometers northeast of Minsk) was pacified . . . In Logoysk 6 partisans and 1 Communist were shot. In Pleshchenitsky 52 Jews and 2 partisans were shot. In Sucha-Gora, 1 man who had hidden ammunition was shot.

"In the other localities, none of the above named elements were to be found . . .

"On 10/16/41, after spending the night in Logoysk, the towns of Bicholin, Berezina, Volcza . . . were searched. In Volcza a partisan who was out on the street was shot. In the other towns the operation was unsuccessful. (The Jews had already been liquidated by the SD from Borisov) . . .

"On 10/21/41, the 2nd, 4th Co. and 2 companies of Order Police were ordered to search and cleanse Koidanovo (about 40 kilometers southwest of Minsk). 1,000 Jews and Communists were liquidated.

"Fatalities, accidents, illness:

a) fatalities: none

b) accidents: none

Morale of the troops: good."

Document

Commandant of White Ruthenia, Monthly Report dated November 10, 1941 for the period 10/11–11/10/1941.

"During a cleansing operation in the area of Slutsk-Kleck, the 11th Reserve Police Battalion shot: 5,900 Jews."

## The *Wehrmacht* joins in the murders

"Operation Jew-free" was only the prelude to the large-scale ghetto murders. Between October 20, 1941 and December 20, 1941, 60,000 to 80,000 Jews were murdered in the General Commissariat White Ruthenia and in the rear area of Army Group Center. Orders were given and carried out primarily by Himmler's Security Police and the Security Service (SD). But the *Wehrmacht* was actively involved, generally supported by the local auxiliary police forces, which had been established in the meantime by the Germans.

• it supplied the trucks to transport Jews,
• it provided troops to round up victims and cordon off areas,
• it detailed engineers to cover mass graves with explosive charges,
• it provided units which served as execution squads.

The following companies of Infantry Regiment 727 were involved, for example, in executions in the General Commissariat White Ruthenia:

• October 30, 1941, Niesvicz ghetto: 4,500 Jews murdered by the 8th Company;

• November 2, 1941, Lachovichi ghetto: 1,000 Jews murdered by the 8th Company;

• November 5, 1941, ghettos in Yaremichi, Svierzna, Turec: 1,000 Jews murdered by the 8th Company;

• November 9, 1941, Mir ghetto: 1,500–1,800 Jews murdered by the 8th Company;

• November 13–14, 1941, Slonim ghetto: 9,000 Jews murdered by SD and police, aided by the 6th Company;

• December 8, 1941, Novogrudok ghetto: 3,000 Jews murdered by SD and police, aided by the 7th Company.

(Data compiled by the *Zentrale Stelle Ludwigsburg*)

1–4: Mass shootings by the *Wehrmacht*

2

3

4

Minsk ghetto: A transit camp for annihilation

With 100,000 prisoners, the ghetto in Minsk was the largest in the occupied Soviet Union, and it also existed for the longest period – until the autumn of 1943.

Of the 85,000 local Jews and the 15,000 German Jews deported to Minsk, no more than 10,000 survived.

The largest massacres:

• August 1941: 5,000 dead

• November 1941: 19,000 dead

• March 1942: 5,000 dead

• July 1942: 30,000 dead

• October 1943: 4,000 dead

SD and Security Police were responsible for the murders but rather than play the role of a passive onlooker, the *Wehrmacht* participated by cordoning off areas and supplying trucks.

Excerpts from the memoirs of Heinz Rosenberg, a German Jew who survived the Minsk ghetto: "Jahre des Schreckens" ("Years of Terror"), Göttingen 1992

"After all the work details had left the ghetto on July 25, 1942, the entire area was surrounded by SS, *Wehrmacht*, police, NSDAP, and railway troops and the special commando entered the ghetto. Because at the time I was working in the soldiers' barracks and often spent the night there, I knew nothing about what was going on in the ghetto. What we saw in the ghetto in the next few days is indescribable. Even the strongest men broke down, women and children screamed and cried. The cadaverous smell hanging over the camp made everything even worse. The slaughter had been carried out by a SS special commando, but the German *Wehrmacht* soldiers stood guard around the ghetto and watched and made sure that no one could run away and escape death.

"The surviving German Jews from the Special Ghetto 2 had to be housed in our section. Many of these people who were the sole survivors in their families later died of grief and sorrow.

"On the day after the massacre, the details working outside the ghetto had to go to work as usual. The task of clearing the ghetto of corpses fell to those who did not work outside the ghetto. It took them days. Again and again, they found members of their own families and friends among those ripped apart by machine guns. It was simply horrible."

1: Heinz Rosenberg.

2: Mass grave.

**Abt. VII**
**Militärverwaltung**

OKV.R. Dr. Füßlein

Stadtbeauftragter für die Stadt Woroschilowak u.Vertr. d.Abt.-Leiters:
Kriegsverwaltungsrat Melcher

Sachbearbeiter und Büroleitung:
Kriegsverwaltungsoberinspektor Bobe

Sachbearbeiter b.Stadtbeauftragten:
Kriegsverwaltungsinspektor Puschmann

Dolmetscheraufgaben der Abt. VII:
Sonderfhr.Stein, Sonderfhr.Hentzelt

Dolmetscheraufgaben b.Stadtbeauftr.:
Sonderfhr. Hasselblatt

Organis. d. Militärverw.einschl.Personalien d.Militärverwaltungsbeamten

Ausübung d.vollz. Gewalt gegenüber Zivilbevölkerung u.landeseig.Behörden, Erlass v.Rechtsverordnungen

Politische Angelegenheiten,Presse, Rundfunk,Propaganda ( mit Ic )

Aufbau und Beaufsichtigung aller landeseigenen Behörden

Innere Verwaltung

Polizeiliche Angelegenheiten,Organisation d.Hilfspolizei ( mit Ia )

Feuerwehr,ziviler Luftschutz

Volksdeutsche

( ndermassnahmen gegen Juden

Zulassung u. Kennzeichnung ziviler Kraftfahrzeuge

Verkehrswesen (mit Strassentransportstellen)

Strassenwesen (mit Stopi)

Bauwesen und Baupolizei

Religionspolitik,kirchl.Angelegenh.

Schulwesen,Kunst,Wissenschaft

Museen,Archive,Bibliotheken

Betreuung der Zivilbevölkerung

Fürsorgewesen,Sozialversicherung

Gesundheitswesen (mit IVb)

Veterinärwesen (mit IVc)

Finanz- und Steuerwesen
Versorgungsbetr.,sonst.gemeindl.Einr
Zivile Sprachmittler
Zusammenarbeit m.Wi-Dienststellen in allen wirtsch.Angelegenheiten

3: This list summarizes the responsibilities of Section VII of the Military Administration including firefighting, public health and "Special measures against Jews."

Orsha: The establishment and liquidation of a ghetto

The ghetto in Orsha, in the rear area of Army Group Center, was established in September 1941 by the local military headquarters. The ghetto existed until November 20, when an SD commando came and, with the help of units from the local headquarters, shot all 1,750 Jews detained there.

The officer responsible for the ghetto, Paul Eick, described these events in testimony before the military tribunal in Minsk on December 18 and 19, 1945:

"In September . . . 1941, Military Administration Headquarters ordered me to establish a ghetto for the Jewish population in Orsha, . . . to move the Russian population from Engels Street and to relocate the Jewish population from the entire city to Engels Street. I accomplished this task over the course of ten days . . ..

"In November 1941, the Commander of Military Administration Headquarters, Colonel Ascheberg, called a secret meeting. Present were: the head of the Economic Command, the Commander of Military Administration Headquarters, and I. In this secret meeting, Commander Ascheberg explained that the SD would soon take over the ghetto in order to liquidate it by shooting [its inhabitants].

1: Paul Eick

"A few days later (on November 19) the head of the SD, *Obersturmführer* Reschke, came to me and asked me to show him the ghetto. I agreed and accompanied Reschke. After familiarizing himself with the ghetto he told me that he would soon let me know when he would liquidate the ghetto. On the evening of the same day, Reschke told me on the telephone that I should cordon off the ghetto the next morning and that I should let no one out of the ghetto. I carried out this order from Reschke. The entire ghetto was sealed off by a chain of guards according to my instructions. The guards included police from the local headquarters, the local (Russian) auxiliary police service, and the auxiliary guards who were under my command. Once the ghetto was sealed off by the guards, the SD came and began the liquidation of the ghetto . . ."

Ghettos were established and "liquidated" throughout the rear area of Army Group Center in the same way as in Orsha. The estimated number of victims from September 1941 to September 1942: 80,000 Jews.

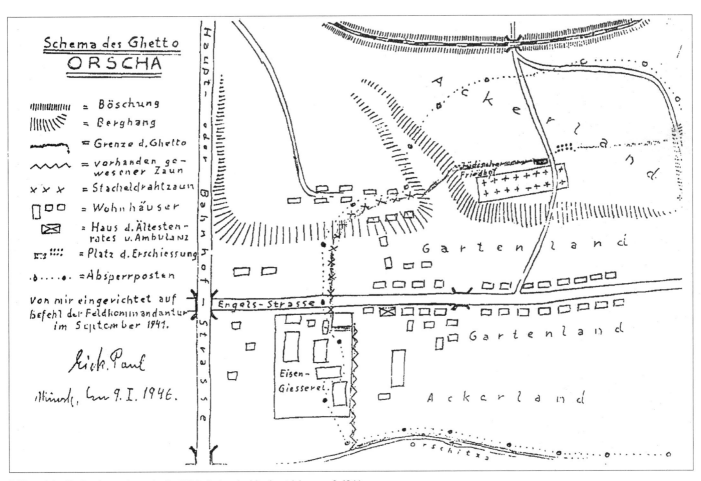

1: Map of the Orsha ghetto drawn by Paul Eick during the Minsk trial, January 9, 1946.

137

# 1943: The end

## Case Study Krasnoye: The end of the *"Arbeitsjuden"*

In the spring of 1943, the murder of Jews doing forced labor for the *Wehrmacht* gradually began. Whereas Himmler insisted on bringing the "Final Solution" to an end, military leaders vacillated: on the one hand, they did not want to do without these work slaves, on the other hand, they did not object if troublesome witnesses disappeared just in time before the great retreat began.

In no case did military commanders oppose the murderous operations of the SD commandos and in most cases they cooperated with the SD.

In Krasnoye, northwest of Minsk, there was a large *Wehrmacht* repair camp, a so-called army ordnance park. 1,500 Jews were employed there and interned on the *Wehrmacht* grounds. The commander had brought part of this work force from a neighboring ghetto in the summer of 1942. The aged and the women and children not fit for work had been executed by *Wehrmacht* soldiers, with support from a SD commando.

In March 1943, the fate of the *"Arbeitsjuden"* in Krasnoye was also sealed. Under the pretense of an immunization, the work columns were driven into a special barracks instead of to work. Those remaining in the ghetto were rounded up by soldiers of the ordnance park. The SD commando awaited both groups, shot them in a nearby barn, and then burned their bodies.

Document

Testimony of the witness Szmuel Palti, former Jewish prisoner in Krasnoye, on 7/18/1967, criminal case at the *Landgericht Bochum*

"On the day in question, the Jews were led to work as usual, as if nothing special was in store. I went to work in a column marching in rows. Higher officers of the ordnance park were already standing at the gate of the park. They were already waiting for us. The higher officers had never waited for us in this way. They told us that we had to receive injections because of typhus in the camp (the camp was immediately behind the ordnance park). We were led there. The gate was closed right behind us and I immediately saw that the entire camp was surrounded by armed Germans . . . We were ordered to go into the barracks and were then ordered to undress down to our underclothing. Women and men were together there. We were held there until the afternoon. Then trucks drove up and they began to drag people out of the barracks in groups. – I saw how they dragged my mother and my younger brother, among others, out of the barracks. The trucks slowly filled with people and then they drove in the direction of the Usha River. There, in a wooden building – the house stood on the bank of the river – the people brought by truck were shot and then burned."

Document

Interrogation of Defendant K., former company head of the 1st Company of Security Battalion 28, on 8/31/1967

"A messenger came to the assembly area south of Krasnoye with the order that I was to go with my unit to the town of Krasnoye and encircle the Jewish ghetto there. I withdrew with my company and fulfilled the order . . . I ordered my men to search this area for Jews and my men turned up several Jews in the search . . . While the Jews and Jewesses were being combed out of the ghetto by my men, Jews were brought under guard with trucks and unloaded. I stood nearby, that is to say in an open place, on a rise. I watched as the Jews were unloaded from the trucks . . ."

"During this part of the operation, the soldiers under my command were charged with cordoning off the site so that Jews could not escape . . . When the operation was finished I gave the order to withdraw. I did not wait until the barn with the dead Jews was set on fire.

"As far as I observed, the Jews were led, usually in fours, into the nearby barn where two to four men with pistols awaited them and killed them with shots in the back of the neck."

Document

Interrogation of F., former Corporal, on 1/16/1969

"Battalion Commander Haferkamp gave a speech with approximately these words: 'Today is a special operation, the Jews are to be bumped off. We don't have anything to do with the shootings, the SS will do that. We only have to cordon off the ghetto. Anything that breaks out must be shot.'"

Document

Interrogation of S., former Corporal, on 9/19/1969

"At the beginning of the operation, some of the *Wehrmacht* units, that is, some from the Security Battalion, and some of the men from the army ordnance park were ordered into the area between the way out of the ghetto and the barn and were told to secure the Jews' path on both sides, to make it impossible for the Jews to escape. Attempts to escape were made. I think that Jews succeeded or might have succeeded in reaching the river bank to dive under. Fleeing Jews were shot at."

Document

Interrogation of the former Commander of Krasnoye, Colonel Z., on 11/11/1964

"In my opinion, the security of the army ordnance park would have been endangered if I had not cordoned off the area. Otherwise, a number of Jews would surely have escaped and joined the partisans. These Jews, who were well acquainted with the army ordnance park, could then have given the partisans exact information about our army ordnance park, about the personnel, etc."

1: Jews in the army ordnance park.

2–3: Jews shot "while escaping" in Krasnoye.

3

Breach of international law

The treatment of Soviet prisoners of war during World War II is, to date, the most evident crime of the German *Wehrmacht.* More than 50 % of those taken prisoner died, 3.3 million out of a total of 5.7 million POWs. In World War I, the death rate of Russian POWs was about 5 %.

The reason for this difference in the numbers of victims was Hitler's intention to wage the war against the Soviet Union as a "war of *Weltanschauung*". In Hitler's view, members of the Red Army were not soldiers drafted to do military service but the active agents of a criminal *Weltanschauung.*

In the "Guidelines for the treatment of Soviet prisoners of war" issued on September 8, 1941, the High Command of the *Wehrmacht* (OKW) drew the consequences : "For these reasons, the Bolshevist soldier has lost every right to treatment as an honorable soldier and in accordance with the Geneva Convention."

The troops were drilled to see a brutal opponent in every unarmed prisoner: every sign of disobedience was considered to be sabotage, every conversation could only be the beginning of a conspiracy, every step out of line was interpreted as an attempt to escape.

The reaction to such behavior: "merciless use of firearms."

1: Columns of captured Red Army soldiers, 1941.

2

3

4

141

## Calculated mass death

The largest number of deaths – about 2 million out of the total of 3.3 million – occurred in the first months of captivity. Hunger and thirst, exhaustion and epidemics were more deadly than the carbines of the German guards. These deaths cannot be explained by arguing – as some still do – that the German authorities had not reckoned with such masses of prisoners and were therefore overwhelmed.

The concept of battles of encirclement was aimed at defeating and imprisoning entire armies. The plans for the treatment of prisoners reveal that mass death was part of the plan:

• No transportation was available for the prisoners. In order to reach the prison camps, they had to march hundreds of kilometers. Anyone who showed signs of exhaustion was shot. Wounded Red Army soldiers experienced the same fate. They were seen as mere ballast.

• There were no barracks or permanent housing. The camps were simply open areas fenced off with barbed wire. The prisoners had to lie in the sun, then in mud, and in the fall – with temperatures as low as minus 30 degrees centigrade – faced the possibility of freezing to death.

• Hunger was the most fatal threat. Daily rations amounted to only one-fourth of what a normal person needed to survive. These meager rations resulted from the decision reached before the campaign, i. e. that providing food for the *Wehrmacht* and for Germany had the highest priority. "As a result, millions of people will surely starve", was the terse conclusion formulated at a conference of German State Secretaries in Berlin in May 1941.

Document

Report by *Ministerialrat* Dorsch to Rosenberg, the Minister for the Occupied Eastern Territories, about his visit to the Minsk camp, 7/10/1941

"The prisoners who are crowded into this place can scarcely move and are forced to relieve themselves where they stand.

"The prisoners of war, who have created a virtually insoluble food supply problem, sometimes go six to eight days without food and, in the animal apathy caused by hunger, have but a single craving: to get something to eat.

"The only possible language which the inadequate guard detachments, who do their duty day and night without relief, can employ is that of the weapon, which is used mercilessly."

1: A POW camp in the Soviet Union, summer 1941.

2–5: Minsk POW camp, summer 1941.

3

4

5

143

## The "selections"

The "Commissar Order" (June 6, 1941) stipulated that the troops "use their weapons immediately to dispose of" every captured commissar of the Russian Army.

Under the assumption that many commissars were hiding among the normal prisoners, the *Wehrmacht* immediately began "combing through camps". In the process, the group of persons included in the definition of dangerous enemies was extended substantially: From July 24 on, "politically intolerable and suspicious elements" were to be singled out and shot. At first, Jews were only supposed to be separated from the other prisoners. In practice, they were usually shot immediately.

The High Command of the *Wehrmacht* (OKW) had reached an agreement with Himmler regarding a division of labor in carrying out these "selections". The *Wehrmacht* was responsible in the battle zone and the army rear areas, while Himmler's *Einsatzgruppen* selected and executed POWs in the camps inside Germany, in the Polish *Generalgouvernement* and in the Reich Commissariats. As of October 1941, these death squads were in operation everywhere and more than half a million prisoners fell victim to them.

**Document**

From the diary of Richard Heidenreich, Private, Infantry Regiment 354, 12th Company

"July 1941. After traveling for several days we arrived in Minsk. Our battalion was assigned the task of guarding 6,000 prisoners and shooting all the Jews in the city. At night, many of the prisoners tried to escape and we had to reach for our weapons. Our battalion alone finished off 500 Jews."

**Document**

Testimony of former Private M., Infantry Regiment 354, 12th Company, during a judicial inquiry on 12/2/1963

"Our company was in the Minsk area. We were responsible for guarding POWs and Jews. It was a very large prison camp. . . . I want to say here that the camp was divided and the Jewish prisoners were separated from the normal POWs.

"While we were there . . . it often happened that in the morning trucks drove up and Jews were taken away with them. They were brought to a hill near Minsk and shot there. . . . The shooting commando was a detachment of the Military Police."

**Document**

Testimony of former Private B., Infantry Regiment 354, 12th Company, in a judicial inquiry, 12/10/1963

"As part of our security responsibilities we had . . . the task of guarding a huge prison camp in Minsk. . . . The prisoners from the Minsk-Bialystok battle of encirclement were in that camp. As far as I know, Jews were detained there as well. I know that these Jews were later shot. Those shot were political commissars of the Russian Army and also other Jews."

**Document**

Testimony of the former Battalion Commander W., who was also commanding officer of the 12th Company of Infantry Regiment 354, to the Criminal Police on 1/28/1964

"Here in Minsk we had to guard a huge prison camp. . . . The prison camp was made up of prisoners from the battles of encirclement in Bialystok and Minsk. There may have been about 120,000 people. . . . Concerning shooting of Jews or of political commissars in the camp, I heard and saw nothing."

1–2: POWs marked as Jews.

2

3–4: Himmler's visit to the Minsk POW camp, July 1941.

4

5–6: The guards in July 1941: Infantry Regiment 354.

6

7–8: Police during executions in the Minsk POW camp.

8

# Winter 1941/42: The end of the *Blitzkrieg*

With the early onset of winter in 1941, the mortality rate rose quickly: In October 1941, 20,000 to 50,000 POWs died in the rear area of Army Group Center, in November the toll was 80,000 to 100,000.

By this time, Hitler had decided to redirect POWs from the camps into the production of armaments. But at least initially, this brought no change in living conditions for the POWs:

• Because of the onset of winter, prisoners were transported by train, but only open freight cars were used. Every fifth prisoner froze to death.

• The only permanent housing available were former Russian barracks and some recently built barracks camps. The POW camp commanders began a process of systematic decimation.

1–9: The Lesnaya POW camp, 150 kilometers west of Minsk, 1941/42.

3

4

5

6

7

8

9

A POW camp commander does his job

Dulag 131, a POW transit camp with several sub-camps, was located in Bobruysk, a town on the western border of the Army Group Center's rear area. In the fall of 1941, approximately 40,000 POWs were detained there, half of them in Camp IV, an old fortress from the time of the Czars. In November 1941, the decision was reached to drastically reduce their number. On December 2, 1945, Carl Languth, Camp Commandant of Camp 4, reported as a defendant before the military tribunal in Minsk on how this operation was carried out:

"Several days before 11/7/41, it may have been 11/4 or 11/5/41, the Commandant of *Dulag 131*, Lieutenant Colonel Freiherr von Roeder, while visiting Camp I, discussed the following with me in my room: 'As you know, the camps are overcrowded, railroad cars or other means of transporting the prisoners are not available, in spite of all our efforts. Colonel Sturm (the staff officer for prisoners of war) has received orders from OKW Berlin which provide for the annihilation of prisoners of war in such cases. Camp IV, the barracks, will go up in flames. Prisoners of war will die in the blaze, because they will not all have time to leave the barracks. The fire is to be on 11/7/41, the anniversary of the socialist revolution. Arson by the prisoners of war and an attempt to escape will be simulated. A special detachment chosen by Colonel Sturm will set the fire.' "

The fire was set as agreed. Prisoners fleeing from the building ran into the bullets from four machine guns; 4,000 were killed. The surviving prisoners were sent to other camps in the city. For most of them, it meant only a delay of their death.

Document

Testimony of a defendant in the Minsk trial, Carl Languth, the former Bobruysk Camp Commandant, on 12/28/1945 and 1/25/1946

"While transferring the surviving prisoners into Camp I, I did not keep the guards from shooting at them. I even supported the shooting. A large number of prisoners of war were shot, so that the route was strewn with 500 to 600 corpses. . . .

"After the prisoners of war arrived in Camp I, they were decently housed. On the same day, 2,000 prisoners from Camp I were sent on foot to Slutsk. As was reported to me later, only a few of these 2,000 prisoners of war reached Slutsk. Escorting soldiers reported that the prisoners of war tried to escape when they passed through a forest and were shot by the guards."

Document

Testimony of defendant Carl Languth, former Commandant of the Bobruysk POW camp, in the Minsk trial, January 25, 1946

"I don't exactly remember when it was, but I think that in December 1941 the Division provided fifty train cars for our use. And we loaded the prisoners of war into these cars."

District attorney:
"How many prisoners of war were transported in open cars?"

"3,200 prisoners of war."

District attorney:
"Are you aware that all prisoners of war who were transported in open freight cars in December 1941 froze and that their corpses were thrown down the embankment?"

"I was told that by witnesses."

District attorney:
"How often were prisoners of war transported in this way during the winter?"

"Often."

1–2: Murdered Soviet POWs.

2

3–4: The Bobruisk POW camp.

4

5: Defendants in the Minsk trial.

From the photo album of Kurt Wafner

Kurt Wafner, born in 1918 in Berlin, assistant in a physics laboratory, anarchist and anti-war activist, was drafted into a territorial defense battalion in 1941. Assigned to duty in Minsk, he guarded POWs in the Masjukovtshina camp. Because of poor vision, he was assigned to indoor duty only. In late June 1943 he was declared unfit for service and sent home, where he worked in the armament industry in Berlin.

Wafner did not take photographs himself, but bought pictures – "usually for a little tobacco" – from fellow-soldiers in his own or other units.

2: Minsk

3: "Russian prisoners of war"

1: Kurt Wafner

7: "In front of the company kitchen in the forest camp"

8: "Room in the Pushkin Barracks"

12: "Vera"

13: "Murdered partisans in Minsk, 1941"

150

150

4–5: "Prison barracks in the forest camp"

5

6: "Transporting corpses in the forest camp"

9: "Column of prisoners in the forest camp"

10: "Road construction work in the forest camp"

11: "Women in Minsk"

14: "Mass grave with Russian prisoners of war"

15–16 "Prisoners of war who were shot in the forest camp"

16

Declaration of war against the civilian population

According to the rules of international law, the population of an occupied country was subject to martial law. Under certain conditions, civilians who exercised armed resistance were to be dealt with as soldiers. The High Command of the *Wehrmacht* annulled all of these ties to international law before the campaign against the Soviet Union began: the military courts were relieved of their responsibility for the civilian population and the troops became the legal authority (Order of May 13, 1941).

The troops were under orders to shoot irregulars immediately – "in battle or while escaping." Not only armed civilians counted as irregulars, but unarmed persons as well: "rabble-rousers, pamphleteers, arsonists" or those merely "suspected" of such deeds.

If it was impossible to determine individual perpetrators or suspected perpetrators, "collective reprisal measures", meaning the shooting of hostages or the burning of entire villages, were implemented automatically.

It is therefore false to assume that the *Wehrmacht* battle against the partisans was waged as a normal military battle against armed groups. The orders from spring and summer 1941 and the troops' actual practices immediately after the assault on Russia were tantamount to a declaration of war against the entire civilian population and thus created the conditions which led to the development of a partisan movement in 1942/43.

Document

The Führer and Supreme Commander of the *Wehrmacht*
Decree
concerning military jurisdiction in the "Barbarossa" area and concerning special measures of the troops

The jurisdiction of the *Wehrmacht* serves primarily to maintain military discipline.

Due to the great size of the operational area in the East, the type of combat operations required to suit these conditions, and the special nature of our opponent, the *Wehrmacht* courts face tasks which, for as long as combat continues and until the captured territories have been pacified, and with their limited personnel, they will only be able to fulfill under the prerequisite that they limit their work to their main task.

This goal can only be realized if the troops defend themselves mercilessly against every threat posed by the hostile civilian population

Therefore, the following regulations will apply in the "Barbarossa" area (operations area, Army Group Rear Area, and area of political administration):

Dealing with criminal acts by hostile civilians.

1. Criminal acts by hostile civilians are withdrawn from the jurisdiction of courts-martial and summary courts-martial until further notification.

2. The troops are to kill irregulars mercilessly in battle or while escaping.

3. All other attacks by hostile civilians against the *Wehrmacht,* its personnel and entourage are to be repressed by the troops on the spot with the most extreme measures, including annihilation of the attacker.

4. Wherever the application of such measures was neglected or was not immediately possible, suspicious elements are to be brought before an officer as soon as possible. The officer will decide whether they are to be shot. If conditions do not permit a rapid identification of individual perpetrators, collective reprisal measures are to be carried out summarily against towns from which the Army was attacked insidiously or treacherously, by order of an officer with the rank of a battalion commander or higher.

5. It is expressly forbidden to detain suspicious perpetrators for the purpose of turning them over to the courts, upon the reestablishment of jurisdiction over inhabitants of the country.

6. Commanders-in-chief of the Army Groups can reintroduce, by mutual agreement with the responsible commanders of the Air Force and of the Navy, *Wehrmacht* jurisdiction over civilians in areas which have been sufficiently pacified.

For the area of political administration, this order is issued by the Chief of the High Command of the *Wehrmacht*

**Document**

Notes on legal points of the Führer's Decree of 5/13/1941, from the Activity Report 2 of *Panzer* Group 3, 8/19/1941

"After reading the Führer's Decree, Lieutenant General Müller explained that in the coming campaign the necessities of war would, under some circumstances, take priority over one's sense of justice . . .

"The definition of an irregular includes a civilian who obstructs the German *Wehrmacht* or who calls for obstruction (e.g. agitators, pamphleteers, not obeying German orders, arsonists, destroying signs, supplies, etc.) . . .

"In cases where the perpetrator is not clearly identified, suspicion will often have to suffice. Often there is no clear proof. Drastic collective measures such as burning to the ground, shooting a group of people, etc. Troops should, however, not let themselves be diverted or act out of blood lust. No unnecessary agitation, only as needed for the security of the troops and for the rapid pacification of the country."

Geheime Kommandosache!

Heeresgruppe B
Ic/A.O.Nr.15/41 g.Kdos.Chefs.

Eilt! Chefsache!
Nur durch Offizier!

H.Qu., den 13. 6. 41
25 Ausfertigungen
25. Ausfertigung.

Betr.: Verfügung CKH., General z.b.v. beim Ob.d.H. ( Gruppe R.Wes. ) Nr. 80/41 g.K.Chefs., v.24.5.41.

Zusätze der Heeresgruppe B:

1.) Die mündliche Bekanntgabe des Führererlasses über den Rahmen der Kommandeure mit eigener Gerichtsbarkeit hinaus hat wie folgt zu erfolgen:

   a) Offiziere bis zum Batl.-Kdr. abwärts  -  Teil I;
   b) alle Offiziere  -  Teil I, Ziffer 1, 2, 3, 4-1.Abs.,5;
   c) Unteroffiziere u. Mannschaften  -  Teil I, Ziff. 1 - 3

2.) Unter " Freischärler " sind alle feindliche Zivilpersonen zu verstehen, die in irgendeiner Form Gewaltmassnahmen gegen die Truppe ausüben ( Betätigung mit der Waffe oder gefährlichen Werkzeugen, Sabotage usw. ).
   Der Art. II der Haager Landkriegsordnung, wonach der Bevölkerung eines Landes für den Fall, dass sie keine Zeit gehabt hat, sich zu organisieren, das Recht eingeräumt wird, sich gegen einen eindringenden Gegner zu verteidigen, findet bei kommenden Einsatz keine Anwendung.

3.) Hinsichtlich der Behandlung von Straftaten von Angehörigen der Wehrmacht und des Gefolges gegen Landeseinwohner ändert sich bei der Truppe selbst durch den Führererlass nichts; d.h. Tatberichte sind in den gleichen Fällen wie bisher - unter Berücksichtigung des § 16 a der H.Dv. 3/13 (KSSVO)- einzureichen.
   Der Gerichtsherr entscheidet, ob ein kriegsgerichtliches Verfahren einzuleiten ist oder nicht.
   Massgebend für diese Entscheidung des Gerichtsherrn ist die Aufrechterhaltung der Manneszucht.

Supplements to Hitler's decree regarding the exercise of military jurisdiction, issued by Army Group B on June 13, 1941. The supplement suspends Article II of the Hague Convention on Land Warfare with respect to combat against partisans and provides that crimes committed by soldiers against civilians are only to be subject to punishment if they violate the norms of discipline ["*Manneszucht*"].

## Stragglers

The aim of the *Blitzkrieg* against the Soviet Union was to penetrate as far as possible into the country in three spearheads and to annihilate the majority of enemy troops in huge battles of encirclement. As a result of this strategy, parts of the Russian Army were overtaken by German troops without a battle and encircled units were able to escape into the forests.

Very few Russian soldiers responded to the *Wehrmacht's* call to surrender and hand over weapons: The practice of shooting prisoners following interrogation and reports of masses dying in the camps acted as deterrents. Instead, "stragglers" attempted to break through to their own troops or simply to go underground. The fact that part of the population provided stragglers with food, clothing, and medicine – voluntarily or thanks to the use of force – served as a welcome confirmation of the image of an insidious and brutal enemy propagated in the orders and guidelines of the *Wehrmacht* leadership before the campaign began:

• Armed partisans lurked in the forests.

• The population was the disguised civilian arm of this force.

• Jews acted as middlemen and spies.

• The entire movement, moreover, was controlled by Moscow.

1–3: Photos by the Propaganda Companies with original captions: "Two Bolshevist soldiers disguised as peaceful civilians were unearthed in a grain field. The work of these snipers and saboteurs is being relentlessly suppressed. Date: 6/28/1941."

2

3: "Civilians who were probably active as snipers are interrogated. Date: 6/28/1941."

4–6: Red Army stragglers, arrested as supposed partisans.

5

6

## The "New System": control, hang, and shoot

Stalin's attempts to initiate and organize a partisan movement in the summer of 1941 soon failed. Thus, in their first year of occupation, the German forces fought a battle against partisans that did not exist, fighting instead against scattered Red Army soldiers who merely wished to survive, and against a defenseless civilian population who anxiously waited to see whether Moscow would fall or the Red Army would return.

The fact that these victims were civilians is most clearly substantiated by the discrepancies between the number of "partisans" killed and German losses. Two examples:

• In the entire rear area of the Army Group Center, 80,000 "partisan" deaths and 3,000 German losses were reported during the first year of occupation.

• In the course of "Partisan Operation Bamberg", which took place in the spring of 1942 in the southern corner of White Russia, 3,500 "partisans and accomplices" were shot. The Germans reported 6 dead and 10 wounded.

During this period, the situation in the occupied territory was characterized by absolute control, constant executions, and ubiquitous gallows.

This situation corresponded to the policy of the *Wehrmacht* leadership, which, in an order dated July 23, 1941, called upon the troops "to spread the kind of terror which is the only suitable means of suppressing any inclination towards resistance in the population."

1–8: Minsk and vicinity: Absolute control of the civilian population.

2

3

4

5

6

8

7

157

Judgement of the *Landgericht Kassel* in the criminal trial of L. and P. 1/9/1963

"After the arrival of the Police Battalion in Minsk, the following occurred, according to the undisputed report of defendant L.:

"The defendant went to staff headquarters of the 707th Infantry Division and reported to the First General Staff Officer there and later to the division commander . . .

"After reporting to the division, the defendant happened onto a crowd of people in Minsk. He witnessed the hanging of two local men and a woman by the Intelligence Officer of the 707th Infantry Division.

"Because they had smuggled several Russian prisoners of war out of a hospital after their recovery and brought them to the partisans, the persons in question were summarily hanged without trial to warn the rest of the population, . . .

"The assumption was widespread in the Germany *Wehrmacht* at the time that the partisans in the occupied Eastern territories were largely lead and supported by Jews, thanks to their intelligence. This belief was also widespread in the 707th Division . . ."

1–7: The public hanging of "partisans" in Minsk, October 1941 described in the judgement of the *Landgericht Kassel*.

2

158

3

4

5

Wir sind Partisanen
und haben auf deutsche
Soldaten geschossen

Мы партизаны, —
СТРЕЛЯВШИЕ ПО
ГЕРМАНСКИМ
ВОЙСКАМ

6

7

1–13: House searches, interrogation and execution of suspicious persons, central Russia, December 1941. Photo by the Propaganda Companies.

2

3

6

7

8

4

5

9

10

11

12

13

# 1942: The partisan threat

## Himmler's new function

German terror produced results. The weak resistance movement, which numbered a mere 30,000 partisans at the end of 1941, had grown to about 150,000 members by the summer of 1942. Most of the partisans operated in White Russia. Their attacks on supply lines and acts of terror against collaborators hindered military operations for the first time and threatened to disrupt the collection of compulsory levies in rural areas.

This was Himmler's hour. In the summer of 1942, he was entrusted with centralizing the war against the partisans. His first official act was to introduce new language usage: from now on, the term to be used was "bandits", rather than partisans and the battle against partisans was now called "combating bandits."

Himmler's second measure was to appoint "a Plenipotentiary for Combating Bandits" who was ordered to begin a constant crusade against the partisans, in cooperation with SS and police formations.

To brutalize this battle, Himmler ordered the deployment of the "Dirlewanger Special Battalion", a troop of criminals who were transported directly from concentration camps to the front. The entire population, including children, was now expressly named as the enemy. A report on the status of the enemy dated November 19, 1942 listed the following as enemy groups:

"Bandits, residents suspected of being bandits or being sympathetic to bandits, Jews and Gypsies, every person on horseback, and youths who appeared to be acting as scouts or lookouts."

The results were as expected: during the large scale operations undertaken under the direction of the SS, SD, and police in the autumn of 1942 in the section of White Russia under civilian administration, the number of persons shot as partisans and "suspected partisans" averaged between 3,000 and 10,000. Each time, up to 30 villages were burned to the ground. A special feature of this method was that the remaining ghettos were destroyed under the cover of these "operations".

**Documents**

Letter from SS-Obergruppenführer K. von Gottberg to SS-Obergruppenführer M. Herff after the conclusion of "Operation Hamburg", 12/21/1942

"My second operation, 'Hamburg' has for the most part come to an end. The result to date –

Enemy dead:
bandits: 1,674,
suspected bandits: 1,510
Jews: 2,958
Gypsies: 30
Total: 6,172.
Unfortunately, 7 German policemen were killed, 10 wounded, and 7 men from the local auxiliaries wounded . . ."

Letter from SS-Obergruppenführer K. von Gottberg to SS-Obergruppenführer M. Herff after the conclusion of "Operation Hornung", 3/8/1943

"Operation Hornung has had the following results –

Enemy dead:
bandits: 2,219;
suspected bandits: 7,378;
prisoners: 65;
Jews shot: 3,300;
own losses –
Germans:
2 dead, 12 wounded;
local auxiliaries:
27 dead, 26 wounded . . ."

1–5: "Dirlewanger" Special Battalion at work: 1: far left: *SS-Oberführer* Oskar Dirlewanger.

The end of scruples

Because of the increase in partisan attacks, troop commanders and commanding officers increasingly criticized the continuation of the terror operations. Himmler's merciless "war on bandits" and unambiguous orders from *Wehrmacht* leaders put an end to that.

"1. In its bandits' war the enemy is using fanatic, Communist-trained fighters who will not hesitate to perpetrate any act of violence. More than ever, the question is now – to be or not to be. This battle has nothing to do with soldierly chivalry or with the agreements of the Geneva Convention . . .

"In this war with no holds barred, the troops are thus legitimated and duty-bound to employ every means, even against women and children, if they are successful . . .

"2. No German involved in the war against the bandits may be subject to disciplinary action or to a court-martial for his behavior in the war against the bandits and their accomplices."

(Order of the OKW, December 16, 1942)

From now on, the *Wehrmacht* followed Himmler's course: Because the partisans were very difficult to capture, suspected partisans were the focus of attention. Villages were occupied, the inhabitants shot or deported to Germany for forced labor. Then the settlements were set on fire.

1–4: Deportation to Germany.

2

3

4

Albert Rodenbusch, recruit in Training Regiment 635, reports on his first action in December 1942, testimony in the Minsk Trial, 1/23/1946

"On the evening of December 29, 1942, we began the operation in a village. There were absolutely no partisans there. The inhabitants of the village had provided warm quarters for us and had fed us. We were astonished when the company commander then ordered us to bum down the village and to arrest the inhabitants. We arrested about fifty persons at that time . . .

"Then we went to another village that was about ten or eleven kilometers from the first one. When we approached this village we were fired on with rifles. The company commander ordered us to take the village and to shoot everyone who resisted or tried to save themselves by escaping . . .

"Then we went to a third village. We found no partisans there, but burned the village down nonetheless and shot fifty inhabitants, among them women and children. The next day we came to a fourth village. Here we carried out the same operation as in the other villages. In this operation one hundred civilians were killed. The village was burned down and eighty persons arrested, whom we took with us."

Burchard, an officer of the Bobruysk Station Headquarters, reports on a normal "cleansing action", testimony in the Minsk Trial, 1/23/1946

"I think it was early July 1942 . . . The village of Kosulichi, Kirovsk County, was surrounded by SS men and the population was driven out of its cottages. I took out my pistol and took part in the action. All citizens had to line up. With the exception of the mayor's family and families of policemen, they were led to the edge of the village and driven into the mill, then the mill was set on fire. We shot those who attempted to flee on the spot. I saw SS men push or simply throw children and old people into the burning mill."

1–5: Occupation of the villages.

2

3

4

5

6: Executed "suspicious" villagers and perpetrators of the murders, including, from left: *Wehrmacht* officer, non-commissioned officer, officer of an allied army, two members of the SD, five members of the police.

## Brothers in arms

In 1943, the struggle against the partisans became a real war. One proof of this change was the fact that the High Command of the *Wehrmacht* (OKW) placed the "war against bandits" in the same category as normal warfare and required troop commanders to deploy all available forces to fight on this front. Furthermore, heavy weapons, tanks and airplanes were deployed in the battle against partisans.

What had once been an exception now became the rule – the combined deployment of large detachments of the SS, the SD, the police, and the *Wehrmacht*.

## Dead zones

According to propaganda claims, the *Wehrmacht* had occupied the Soviet Union with the aim of creating "a new order". The reality was this: Entire regions were labeled as "bandit-infected", depopulated and transformed into dead zones.

The following two documents illustrate the process of "ethnic cleansing," focusing on the Mamayevka area. The proposal described here was made on January 1, 1943:

"After thorough examination of the situation the battalion therefore proposes the creation of a broad no-man's-land between the woods around Mamayevka and the roads between Lopasna – Mglin – Divoka – Potshep . . .

"The area recommended for evacuation encompasses . . . a total of 15 communities with 25,934 inhabitants."

(Report of Security Battalion 791 to the 221st Security Division, January 1, 1943)

Half a year later the task had been accomplished:

"1.) The evacuation of the designated area was accomplished without incident. The population was evacuated with its personal effects and immovable property . . .

"3.) After early depression, the mood improved during the transport, because provisions and transportation were available at the assembly points. Initial fears of being shot were dispelled thanks to these welfare measures . . .

"5.) Since the region marked in red was destroyed by fire, the bandits have been deprived of sources for provisions and hiding places. We have now created clear-cut conditions for the troops in these areas, i. e. every person found in these areas is to be considered a bandit. Cases of mistaken identity and consideration for the civilian population are out of the question here."

(Report on the discharge of duty by Security Regiment 930 to the 221st Security Division, June 23, 1943)

**Document**

Outcome report on the results of "Operation Cottbus" by SS *Hauptsturmführer Wilke*, 6/18/1943

"Enemy losses – in combat: 5,650,
disposed of: 3,616,
prisoners: 552.
The total enemy losses thus come to: 9,818 men.

178 bandit camps and 422 bunkers were destroyed.
2,812 male workers and 450 female workers were registered [erfaßt, i.e., deported as forced laborers].

Taken as booty:
73 wagons,
760 horses,
3,196 cows and calves,
53 pigs,
2,182 sheep,
1,618 hides,
663.03 tons of grain."

**Document**

Report on the agricultural yields of "Operation Cottbus", by District Agricultural Officer Wortmann, 6/12/1943

"The farther we advanced into Russian territory, the more difficult our work became. The villages were uninhabited and there was no livestock. However, 70–80 % of the fields were planted, especially with rye . . .

"The work was made especially difficult for us because the people who had returned to their villages had been shot and the villages burned to the ground. . . .

"In terms of the collection process, the entire operation was not as successful as it could have been. It was striking how the *Wehrmacht*, the police and the SD and the other units involved organized whatever was available to be organized."

1–3: Combined military operations by *Wehrmacht*, police, SS, and SD, winter 1943/44.

3

2

To create clear-cut conditions – that was the aim of the *Wehrmacht* generals and troop commanders when they crossed the borders of the Soviet Union on June 22, 1941. According to their interpretation, that meant achieving a speedy and total victory.

Now, two years later, the aims had been reformulated: To wage war against an entire people with the goal of annihilation. This had been Hitler's intention from the beginning. The *Wehrmacht* of 1943 had finally become his *Wehrmacht*.

1–6: Combined military operations of the *Wehrmacht*, police, SS, and SD, winter 1943/44.

2

3

4

5

6

Bernd Boll, Hannes Heer, Walter Manoschek, Christian Reuther, Hans Safrian **The Iron Cross**

## Inside the heart of darkness

The centerpiece of the exhibition, as it has been shown in Germany and Austria, is an installation in the form of the Iron Cross, the medal for bravery which has been awarded by the German military since 1813. The 330 photos reproduced in this chapter are displayed on the inner panels of this installation. These photographs illustrate the fact that acts of terror perpetrated against prisoners of war, Jews, and other civilians occurred routinely and on a large scale. Moreover, these documents convey the message that in this war, war crimes were not an exception to the rule but themselves the rule, that they were not a means to an end but themselves the goal of war. The creators of these photographs are also present in their images — laughing, triumphant, or businesslike and cold while fulfilling their duty. This place is, in my opinion, at the center of Hitler's *Wehrmacht* — one is standing inside the "heart of darkness".

Hannes Heer

# Tormenting Jews

1–2: Reich Labor Service (RAD), assigned to the *Wehrmacht*, unidentified locality, USSR.

2

3: Jews as forced laborers, clearing rubble, Warsaw, Poland, September 1939. Photo by the Propaganda Companies.

4: Resettlement of Jewish inhabitants from the *Warthegau* to the *Generalgouvernement*.

5: Unidentified locality, Poland.

6: Warsaw ghetto, 1942.

7–8: Jews construct air-raid trenches under the supervision of the Reich Labor Service, Uniejów, Poland, May 1941. Photos by the Propaganda Companies.

8

9: Devastation of the Jewish cemetery in Salonika, Greece; path paved with gravestones.

10–15: Humiliation of Jewish forced laborers, unidentified locality, USSR.

11

12

13

14

15

16: Jewish forced laborers unload artillery shells from a munitions train under *Wehrmacht* supervision. Izbica, Poland, June 28, 1941. Photo by the Propaganda Companies.

17: Kielcę, Poland.

18: Jewish forced laborers unload *Wehrmacht* ammunition crates, Izbica, Poland, July 3, 1941. Photo by the Propaganda Companies.

19–26: Unidentified locality, USSR or Poland.

20

21

22

23

24

25

26

27–30: Humiliation and abuse of the Jewish population of Salonika, Greece, July 11, 1942.

28

29

30

31: Sandomierz, Poland.

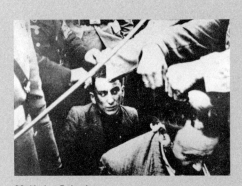

32: Kielcę, Poland.

33: Jarostaw, Poland.

34: Tomaszów Mazowiecka, Poland, photo taken in the period 1939–1941.

35: Western Ukraine, early July 1941. Photo by the Propaganda Companies.

36: Unidentified locality, USSR or Poland.

1: Unidentified locality, USSR, 1942.

2: Unidentified locality, USSR or Poland.

3: Unidentified locality, USSR, October 1941.

4–5: Unidentified locality, USSR.

5

6: Found in the possessions of a German soldier in the Ukraine, February 1944.

7: Unidentified locality, Ukraine, found in the notebook of Corporal Hölzl from Fürth.

8: Porchnov district USSR.

9: Unidentified locality, USSR or Poland.

10: From the album of a German non-commissioned officer, Fritz Lawen, 12th Company of Field Regiment 679. Caption: "They didn't want to work for Germany." Album confiscated by Soviet soldiers. Unidentified locality, USSR.

11: Unidentified locality, USSR. Photo by the Propaganda Companies.

12: From a photo album found in Königsberg, East Prussia, 1945, with the notation "Belorussia 1943." Caption: "Partisan."

13–14: Hanging of the 17-year-old Lepa Radid in Bosanska Krupa, Bosnia, January 1943.

14

15–16: Unidentified locality, USSR.

16

17–23: Velizh, Smolensk area, USSR.

18

19

20

21

22

23

24–26: Unidentified locality, USSR. Photo by the Propaganda Companies.

25

26

27: From the wallet of a German soldier, unidentified locality, USSR.

28–29: Unidentified locality, USSR or Poland.

29

30: From the wallet of a German soldier. Note on the back: 11/3/41 Teploye. Writing on the sign next to the victim: "120 shells in the bag", USSR.

31: Orel, USSR, February 1942. Note on the back: "Hanged on the main street in Orel for refusing to work and committing sabotage. February, 1942."

32–33: Unidentified locality, USSR or Poland.

33

34: Unidentified locality, USSR. From the wallet of a German soldier killed in action.

35: Unidentified locality, Serbia.

36–37: Unidentified locality, USSR.

37

38: Unidentified locality, USSR or Poland.

39: Pančevo (Serbia), April 22, 1941.

40: Unidentified locality, USSR. From the wallet of a German soldier killed in action.

41: Pančevo (Serbia), April 22, 1941.

42: Unidentified locality, USSR.

43: Unidentified locality, USSR or Poland, found by Soviet soldiers near the town of Naumburg.

44–47: Unidentified locality, USSR.

45

46

47

48: Unidentified locality, USSR. Photo by the Propaganda Companies.

49: Unidentified locality, Serbia, spring 1941. Handwritten note on the front: "Tree blossoming in Serbia."

50: Unidentified locality, Poland.

51: Brest, White Russia.

52: Minsk, White Russia, 1941.

53: Novgorod area, USSR, 1944.

54: Near Minsk, White Russia, 1942/43.

55: Unidentified locality, USSR.

56: Kiev, Ukraine.

57: Minsk, White Russia, Park on Karl Marx Street, October 26, 1941.

58–59: Unidentified locality, USSR.

59

60: Minsk, White Russia.

61: Perlez, Voivodina.

62: Minsk, White Russia, November 6, 1941.

63: Mogilev, White Russia.

64: Unidentified locality, Serbia.

65: Unidentified locality, USSR or Poland.

66: Unidentified locality, USSR. Photo by the Propaganda Companies.

67: Velizh, Smolensk region, USSR.

68: Along the Minsk-Borisov road of advance, White Russia 1942/43.

69: Unidentified locality in the Ukraine. From the wallet of Corporal Hölzl.

70: Kharkov area, Ukraine, time period 1941–1943. Corpse of a collective farmer, Tichon Dimitrievič Danilin.

71: Kharkov area, Ukraine, occupied from 1941–1943. Corpses of the collective farmers Timofej Il'ic Aljab'eev and Andrej Sidorivič Saratov.

72: Stalingrad area, USSR.

73: Unidentified locality, USSR.

74: From the wallet of a German soldier. Note on the back: "Russia."

75: Unidentified locality, USSR or Poland.

76: Unidentified locality, USSR or Poland, found by Soviet soldiers in the village of Zotwiz.

77: Ukraine, 1941–1943, text on the sign: "Punishment for taking the helmet from the grave of a German soldier."

78: From a photo album, found by Soviet soldiers in Elsterwerda, Dresden district [Kreis].

79–80: From the photo album of the German NCO Fritz Lawen, 12th Company of Field Regiment 679. Caption: "They didn't want to work for Germany." Unidentified locality, USSR.

80

81: From the wallet of the German soldier Fritz Qualmann, prisoner of war. Unidentified locality, USSR or Poland.

185

82: Minsk, White Russia.

83: Unidentified locality, USSR. Photo by the Propaganda Companies.

84: USSR, 1942. Photo by the Propaganda Companies.

85: Unidentified locality, Baltic area.

86: Along the Minsk – Borissov road of advance, White Russia, 1942/43.

87: Minsk, White Russia, Park on Karl Marx Street, October 1941.

88: Voronezh, USSR, October 1941. Text on the sign: "The fate of all partisans who threaten the Russian population and hinder them at peaceful work."

89: Member of the military police in front of a hanged person. Unidentified locality, USSR.

1: Unidentified locality.

2: Bogodukhov, Ukraine. From the wallet of a German soldier.

3: Minsk, White Russia, 1941. Photo by the Propaganda Companies.

4: Orsha, Vitebsk area, White Russia, July 1941.

5: Unidentified locality, USSR. From the wallet of a German soldier.

6–7: Porchnov district, USSR.

7

8: Kharkov or Bogodukhov, Ukraine. From a wallet.

9: Kharkov or Bogodukhov, Ukraine. Caption: "Easter 1943."

10: Unidentified locality, USSR.

11: Unidentified locality, USSR. From a wallet.

12–14: Destruction of tracks with a "rail wolf", Vitebsk area, White Russia, March 1944. Photo of the Propaganda Companies.

13

14

15: Kharkov or Bogodukhov, Ukraine. Caption: "Change of position to [illegible]." From a wallet.

16: Central Russia, December 1941. Photo by the Propaganda Companies.

17: Unidentified locality, USSR, October 29, 1941.

18: Village near Volokhovskiy, Novgorod area, USSR, November 27, 1941.

19: Dnepropetrovsk, USSR, September 1943.

20: Orsha, White Russia, 1944.

21–22: Preparations for blowing up tracks, Grodno, White Russia, July 1944.

22

23: Begoml' area, White Russia.

24–26: Unidentified locality, USSR, 1942/43.

25

26

27: Begoml' area, White Russia.

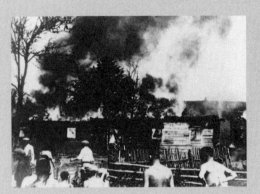

30: Begoml' area, White Russia.

29

28–29: Ostrovok, USSR.

31: Unidentified locality, USSR.

32: Brest area, White Russia, 1941.

33: Unidentified locality.

34: Near Kosovska Mitrovica, Serbia.

35: Porchnov district, USSR.

36: Unidentified locality, USSR. From the wallet of a German soldier. Note on the back: "Easter 43"

37: Unidentified locality.

38: From a photo album, found by Soviet soldiers in Bockau. Caption: "The Ukraine is burning."

39: Unidentified locality, USSR.

40–42: Unidentified locality, USSR. From the wallet of a German soldier.

41

42

43: Village in eastern Bosnia, 1942.

44: Unidentified locality, USSR.

1–4: Čuprija, Serbia, 1941.

2

3

4

5: Čačak, Serbia.

6: Unidentified locality, Serbia.

7: Jajinci, near Belgrade. Inmates of the concentration camp in Banjica, Serbia being shot.

8: Čuprija, Serbia.

9: Unidentified locality.

10: Shooting in Jajinci, near Belgrade, Serbia, 1941.

11–13: Unidentified locality, Poland or USSR.

12

13

14–16: Hostages from the Banjica concentration camp in Jajinci, near Belgrade, Serbia being shot.

15

16

17: Unidentified locality, Poland or USSR.

18: Čuprija, Serbia.

19: Guto-Buino, USSR.

20: Unidentified locality, found in July 1944 on a German soldier killed in action in Brest, White Russia.

21: Unidentified locality, USSR.

22–23: Unidentified locality, USSR.

23

24: Konskie, Poland, September 1939. Caption: "Jews doing work they're not used to."

25–27: Unidentified locality, USSR or Poland.

26

27

29

30

28–30: Zloczow, Ukraine, early July 1941. The photos have been identified with a high probability as showing political prisoners murdered by the Russian secret police NKWD (28) and Jews murdered in reprisal for the NKVD victims after the Germans took the town (29, 30). Photos found in January 1944 in the belongings of Richard Worbs (field post number 31102).

33

31: Zloczow, Ukraine, early July 1941. Jews exhuming bodies of NKVD victims. Photos found in the belongings of a German soldier near Brest, July 1944.

32–34 Zlozcow, Ukraine, early July 1941. Several hundred Jews were forced to exhume the NKVD victims (28,33) and were then shot by German troops (34). Photos from an album belonging to Colonel Otto Korfes, who was stationed at the time with his Infantry Regiment 518 (Infantry Division 295) in Zloczow.

35: Russian POWs shovel their own graves, unidentified locality, USSR.

34

36–38: Mačva region (Serbia), autumn 1941.

37

38

39: Unidentified locality.

40: Unidentified locality.

41: Execution of youths in the Sajmište Semlin camp in Belgrade 1943.

42: Mass execution in Serbia.

43: Execution in Bor, eastern Serbia, 1941.

44–48 Vitebsk region, USSR, May/June 1944. Photos by the Propaganda Companies.

45

46

47

48

49: Unidentified locality, USSR.

50: Unidentified locality, Serbia.

51: Jagodina, Serbia, 1941.

52: Members of the partisan unit of Paraćin before being shot in Ćuprija, Serbia, on November 29, 1941.

53: Captured "Gypsies" from the Šabac area, marching to the Šabac concentration camp, Serbia, September 1941.

54: Partisans from Gornja Mutrica are led to be shot, Ćuprija, Serbia, 1941.

55–57: Hostages are led to be shot, Ćuprija, Serbia, 1941.

56

57

58: Unidentified locality, USSR.

59: Unidentified locality, White Russia.

60: Unidentified locality, Serbia.

61: German punitive expedition in the Šabac area, Serbia, 1941.

62: Borislav, Drogobych area, southwest of L'vov, western Ukraine, May 1942.

63: Riga, Latvia.

65

64–65: Unidentified locality, USSR or Poland.

66: Drogobych, southwest of L'vov, western Ukraine. Inhabitants of the city being shot, Marketplace Nr. 9, August 9, 1944.

69

67: After an execution in the Šabac camp, Serbia.

68–73: Execution of hostages in Condomari, Crete, June 2, 1941.

70

71

72

73

74: Pančevo (Serbia), April 22, 1941.

75: Unidentified locality, Serbia.

76: Unidentified locality, Serbia.

77: Chernigov, Ukraine, 1942.

78–79: Unidentified localities, USSR.

79

1–4: Smolensk POW camp, USSR, August 1941.
Photos by the Propaganda Companies.

2

3

4

5: POWs trade clothing for bread, unidentified
locality, USSR. Photo by the Propaganda
Companies.

6: Šabac concentration camp, Serbia

7: Nikopol POW camp, USSR, 1944.

8: From the wallet of a German soldier. Handwritten
note on the front: "Varena. Prisoners. June 41."

9: Unidentified locality, USSR.

10: From the wallet of a German soldier. Handwritten note on the front: "Prisoners getting bread, to the right Inspector Henke." USSR.

11: Unidentified locality, USSR.

12: Unidentified locality, central Russia, September/October 1942. Signs warn of danger of contracting typhus after entering a Russian home. Photo by the Propaganda Companies.

13: From the wallet of a German soldier. Handwritten note on the front: "Prisoners Varena 7/1/41." USSR.

15

14–15: POW camp near Minsk, White Russia, June/July 1941. Photos of the Propaganda Companies.

16: POWs in the camp at the town of Shepetovka, USSR, February 12, 1944. From the wallet of a German soldier.

17: Smolensk POW camp, USSR, August 1941. Photo of the Propaganda Companies.

18: Kharkov POW camp, Ukraine.

19: Camp N 14, Wärusis work site, USSR, August 1941. POWs pulling a mowing machine. From the wallet of a German soldier.

20–21: Unidentified locality, USSR.

21

22: Minsk-Masjukovtshina POW camp 1941, White Russia.

23–24: From the photo album of Fritz Lawen, German NCO (12th Company of Field Regiment 679). Notation: "Hunger hurts." Unidentified location, USSR.

24

# Deportations

1: Transport to concentration camps, Želenik train station, Yugoslavia, August 26, 1942.

2: Unidentified locality, USSR or Poland.

3: Transfer to the Jasenovac concentration camp, Yugoslavia, about 1942.

4: Deportation to Germany, Kovel train station, Volynsk region, Ukraine, 1942/43.

5: Unidentified locality, USSR.

6: Novgorod region, USSR. Expellees during a halt, under the supervision of the Wehrmacht, December 1941.

7: Smolensk area, USSR. Refugee column leaves the village of Demidov, October 1943.

8: Smolensk area, USSR. Refugee column leaves the village of Demidov, October 1943.

9: Unidentified locality, USSR. Population of an area is evacuated.

11: Vitebsk area, White Russia. Expulsion of the population.

12: Orsha area, White Russia. Military police evacuates inhabitants of a village, November 1943.

10: Bryansk area, the village of Sinisjorki, USSR. Expellees receiving food, August 1943.

13: Novgorod region, south of Lake Il'men', USSR. Evacuation of inhabitants, November 1943.

14: Rostov region, USSR. Deportation of the inhabitants of the village of Voltshenskoje to Germany, February 1943.

15: At the Dnepr crossing, USSR, July 17, 1941.

16–18: Novgorod region, south of Lake Il'men', USSR. Evacuation of the population by train, November 1943.

17

18

19: Unidentified locality, USSR. People awaiting deportation, 1943.

20: Unidentified locality, USSR. Deportation to Germany.

21: Ostrov, USSR. Expulsion of civilians, July 22, 1944.

22: Bryansk area, village of Sinisjorki, USSR. Expellees on the road, August 1943.

23–25: Deportation of Jews from Croatia, June/August 1941.

24

25

26: Deportation, Mogilev district, White Russia.

27–32: Unidentified locality, USSR.

28

29

30

31

32

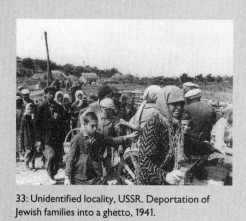

33: Unidentified locality, USSR. Deportation of Jewish families into a ghetto, 1941.

34–36: Unidentified locality, USSR.

35

36

37: Deportation of "Gypsies" to Kozare and Jasenovac, Yugoslavia, July 1942.

38: Preparation for transfer into the Celje concentration camp, Slovenia, 1942.

39: Unidentified locality, USSR. Deportation to Germany.

The exhibition "Vernichtungskrieg. Verbrechen der *Wehrmacht* 1941 bis 1944" ("The German Army and Genocide: Crimes Against War Prisoners, Jews, and Other Civilians, 1941-1944") was first shown in March 1995 in Hamburg as part of a larger project entitled "In the Light, Our Century." The aim of this larger project was to review — fifty years after the end of the Second World War and five years before the end of the century — some aspects of the history of violence in the twentieth century. The exhibition presents the destructivity of war at a level unprecedented in modern times since the Thirty Years War. A further intention of the exhibition was to reveal the precise nature of the organization forced to capitulate unconditionally on May 8, 1945.

The findings shown in the exhibition, and based in part on new material, were not new for historians but had not yet entered the consciousness of a wider public. The results of earlier research were supplemented by new work, producing documents which further substantiated the active role played by the German Army in the Holocaust.

From the beginning, the exhibition attracted great attention. More than one newspaper headlined its report "The End of a Legend", a motto which the exhibition's creators at the Hamburg Institute for Social Research did not themselves choose. It quickly became apparent that the legend created in the 50s of the "unsullied *Wehrmacht*", uninvolved in the crimes of the National Socialist state, is still virulent today. Many German and Austrian cities wanted to host the exhibition and by the fall of 1999, it will have been shown in 33 locations. With a total of approximately 860,000 visitors as of July 1999, it has become the most successful exhibition dealing with contemporary history shown in Germany in the past few decades.

Two factors have contributed to this success. First, contrary to all expectations, the majority of visitors to the exhibition were not representatives of the generation of 35-to 50-year-olds. Instead, there have been surprising

large numbers of young visitors (16- to 30-year-olds) as well as older visitors, i.e., those who experienced World War II as contemporaries, some of them as soldiers. The second factor were the political controversies which erupted as a result of the unexpected success of the exhibition about one year after the first showing. There had been a certain level of public debate on a local or regional level in several of the cities where the exhibition was shown in the first year. Munich, however, marked a turning point and the beginning of a national debate. Peter Gauweiler, a politician and member of the Bavarian Christian Social Union, mobilized not only his fellow party members to protest against the exhibition, but extreme right- wing groups as well, leading to counter-protests and record numbers of visitors to the exhibition. The resulting national controversy about the exhibition culminated in a debate in the German Bundestag, the national parliament, in Bonn on March 13, 1997.

This debate was not only in itself a novelty and curiosity — a parliament debates the pros and cons of an exhibition produced by an academic research institute — but it also demonstrated the emotions that had been aroused by the exhibition. The debate was soon transformed from a more or less ritualistic exchange of pro and con arguments into a forum for personal memories:

"Otto Schily (SPD — Social Democratic Party of Germany): ... My father, an extraordinary entrepreneurial personality, to whom I am infinitely indebted, was a declared opponent of the Nazi Regime. Nevertheless, as a reserve officer who had served in World War I, he was humiliated when he was not called up for military service because of his membership in the Anthroposophical Society, which the Nazis had banned. Only later did he realize the insanity – I'm using his own words – of that standpoint. My wife's father, Jindrich Chajmovic, an unusually courageous and self-sacrificing man, fought as a Jewish partisan in Russia against the German Wehrmacht . Now I'm going to say a sentence that must be accepted by me and by

us all in its severity and clarity: The only person of those I have named here – the only one! – who risked his life for a just cause was Jindrich Chajmovic."[1]

"Freimut Duve (SPD, Social Democratic Party of Germany):... Last week, I was in the strange situation of finding the house in Osijek from which my Jewish grandmother was taken away. I never thought, in the entire 60 years of my life, that I would speak with a woman who saw that happen. We didn't think that anyone was still alive. I spoke with this woman. She described exactly what happened: among the guards there were also German soldiers. But Croatian Ustashas were the ones who threw the old woman, who had a leg handicap, onto a truck. We don't know if she died in Auschwitz or in another camp."[2]

"Christa Nickels (Bündnis 90 / Die Grünen): I want to say that my father was not young when he went to war. He was born in 1908 and died in 1991.    He was not a party member.... Later he was drafted. My mother told me that in the 1950's my father. . .never slept with the window open and screamed terribly in his sleep every night about fire and children. She said that it was simply horrible. Naturally, I loved my father very much. He never told how it was when one shoots at another person for the first time. Today that surprises me.... Several years ago our Chancellor and President Reagan shook hands at a cemetery in Bitburg. Back then I noticed for the first time that my father, in the only photo of him that we have from that time, is wearing a uniform that is black and that has skulls on it. At the time, I was already a representative of the Greens in the Bundestag and didn't dare to ask my father; it was incredibly difficult for me.... In 1989 I traveled to Warsaw with our Green Alliance caucus. 50 years after the attack on Poland we were in Majdanek. I only know that during the war Papa was in France, in Russia, and in Poland. I know that he was taken prisoner in Lemberg. I was in the Majdanek concentration camp and I want you to know that one night I simply broke down because I was terribly shocked by what happened in Majdanek, but just as much by what they did to the men, one of whom was my father. They were for the most part men who loved life and children. It is horrible what they made out of men in this criminal war. Most of them didn't have the strength to extricate themselves from it. All of them made themselves guilty of infinite, atrocious wrongs. The men, women and children – I am the daughter of such a German soldier — are still marked by that today."[3]

How could the "role of the *Wehrmacht* in National Socialism" remain a public taboo for so long, and, at the same time, as we have seen, hover just under the surface, waiting to become an object of public discussion? To answer this question, it is important to remember that immediately after 1945, it was common knowledge that the German *Wehrmacht* as an organization had participated in National Socialist crimes. Konrad Adenauer, who later became the first German Federal Chancellor, wrote to a Catholic priest on February 23, 1946: "The German people ... let themselves be brought into line almost without resistance and in part with enthusiasm. That is where their guilt lies. Furthermore it was known - even if the events in the camps were not known in their entirety - that personal freedom and all legal principles were being trampled on, that grave atrocities were being committed in the concentration camps, that the Gestapo, our SS, and in part also our troops in Poland and Russia were treating the civilian population with unheard-of cruelty.... Therefore, one cannot claim that the public did not know that the National Socialist government and Army leaders were constantly and as a matter of principle violating natural law, the Hague Convention, and the most simple dictates of humanity."[4]

One can probably say that most people were in fact unaware of what went on in the death camps, but reports about the crimes of the *Wehrmacht* made it clear to many people what the fate of the Jewish population of Germany and the rest of Europe was to be — beyond the process of discrimination, deportation, and ghettoization. Gitta Sereny,

in her biography of Albert Speer, quotes a statement made by the attorney who defended Speer during the Nuremberg trials: "One knew that it was dangerous to be a Jew in Hitler's Germany, but one didn't know that it was a catastrophe.[5] I knew absolutely nothing until one day in 1943 when one of my clients, who had served as a medical orderly in Russia, came back with photographs that showed Jews being shot. I advised him to burn or bury them and not to tell anyone what he had seen. And I never told anyone, not even my wife."[6] And one of the visitors to the exhibition relates: "We were in the third or fourth grade and one of the girls came to school one morning making a big fuss and oh, guess what I have, guess what I have, I'll show you later.... During recess she took out these pictures ... and we looked.... What I saw in those pictures was so terrible I could never forget it. Well, there was a post or something and on top was a crossbar or post or something and hanging from it were not just three, four, there were ten, twelve, fifteen prisoners hanging there, all lined up in a row. . . [7]

In the 50's a view spread, one that is still heard today, i.e. that "the *Wehrmacht* had been declared innocent" in the Nuremberg Trial against the so-called major war criminals. Indeed, one of the questions dealt with at the Nuremberg Trials was whether the High Command and the General Staff of the *Wehrmacht* should be declared a criminal organization and formally charged in its entirety as such, as had previously been the case with the SS. A majority of the court's members rejected this proposal, but only because they did not want to characterize the two institutions as "organizations" according to the Charter of the Nuremberg Trials. The argument was that an officer did not join the High Command or the General Staff like a citizen joined the SS. One was drafted into the *Wehrmacht* and rose into the highest military ranks as the result of a military career, which had nothing to do with a decision to join something. The court came to the conclusion that the crimes of the

*Wehrmacht*, which it clearly recognized, were to be documented and punished in individual trials. Independent of this legal decision, the court stated:

> Although the Tribunal is of the opinion that the term " group " in Article 9 must mean something more than this collection of military officers, it has heard much evidence as to the participation of these officers in planning and waging aggressive war, and in committing war crimes and crimes against humanity. This evidence is, as to many of them, clear and convincing.

> They have been responsible in large measure for the miseries and suffering that have fallen on millions of men, women and children. They have been a disgrace to the honourable profession of arms. Without their military guidance the aggressive ambitions of Hitler and his fellow Nazis would have been academic and sterile. Although they were not a group falling within the words of the Charter they were certainly a ruthless military caste ...

> Many of these men have made a mockery of the soldier's oath of obedience to military orders. When it suits their defence they say they had to obey; when confronted with Hitler's brutal crimes, which are shown to have been within their general knowledge, they say they disobeyed. The truth is they actively participated in all these crimes, or sat silent and acquiescent, witnessing the commission of crimes on a scale larger and more shocking than the world has ever had the misfortune to know ...

> Where the facts warrant it, these men should be brought to trial so that those among them who are guilty of these crimes should not escape punishment.[8]

In 1948, during the last of the Nuremberg trials, a case was brought against 14 members of the High Command of the Armed Forces. Two of the officers were sentenced to life imprisonment, nine received sentences of three to twenty years, and two were found innocent. One of the accused committed suicide before the trial began. Several of the sentences were reduced by John McCloy in 1951 and all of the prisoners were released a few years later. Later trials of individual officers of the *Wehrmacht* (such as the one against Erich von Manstein in 1949) hardly affected public consciousness regarding the crimes of the *Wehrmacht*, quite in contrast to the statement on the honor of the *Wehrmacht* soldiers issued by Federal Chancellor Adenauer on April 5, 1951. Adenauer was pressed into making this statement by those members of the *Wehrmacht* who were needed for the establishment of the *Bundeswehr*, the new armed forces of the Federal Republic of Germany and its contribution to NATO, which was founded in 1949. Adenauer emphasized that the Federal Government could not support those truly guilty of war crimes. But the percentage of soldiers in that category was so small that the "honor of the former German *Wehrmacht*"[9] was not tainted. Former professional soldiers had been unjustly held responsible for the lost war; for the most part, they had merely done their duty. "The book must be closed once and for all on the issue of the collective guilt of former professional soldiers."[10]

Furthermore, neither the Nuremberg trials, much less the subsequent trials of individual war criminals can be characterized as attempts to focus on the Holocaust in its entirety. Such a comprehensive perspective on the dimensions of Nazi war crimes began to emerge in the following decades, beginning with the trial of Adolf Eichmann in Jerusalem after being kidnapped by the Israeli Secret Service and with the Auschwitz trials in Frankfurt in 1965. Later, other factors came into play: more widespread knowledge of survivors' reports on German extermination politics; popular presentations which reached large audiences, ranging from the "Holocaust" TV series to Spielberg's Schindler's List; the establishment and expansion of memorials in the Federal Republic of Germany, which occurred mainly in the 70s.

All of these events contributed to turning public attention to the most monstrous aspect of Nazi genocide: systematic mass murder in the death camps. This focus lead people to forget that only some of the murders of European Jews actually occurred in these camps. The other murders, carried out by the SS, the SD, police and *Wehrmacht* units, were overlooked (except by a few historians), because of the more "conventional" methods employed -people were shot, hanged, and beaten to death, not gassed - and because they were perpetrated in the context of seemingly normal acts of war. These murders re-entered public consciousness thanks to the exhibition "The German Army and Genocide."

Clearly, this disappearance from public consciousness served both public and very private needs. Historians concerned with crimes committed under National Socialism focused primarily on specific, clearly defined parts of the population, for the most part institutions or professional groups. The role of industry with respect to slave labor, the role of German banks, of doctors, of lawyers, of specific scientific disciplines had been studied,[11] but fixing one's sights on the *Wehrmacht* meant that the normal citizen became the center of attention. The crimes in the camps had happened "way out there,"[12] there had been relatively few guards, so that when in doubt one could always claim with some degree of plausibility that one had never come in contact with genocide.[13] Furthermore, most people were not members of the professions that had come under scrutiny - in short: one could always claim that while unspeakable crimes had been committed under National Socialism, one had oneself not been affected, nor had one's family.

The discussion about the crimes of the *Wehrmacht* thus automatically became a discussion about the possible links between these crimes and one's own father, grandfather, uncle, or brother. And so people visited the exhibition to search for their relatives on the photos displayed there. Considering the ten million active soldiers on

the Eastern front and the 800 photos shown, this was an irrational pursuit - but one which was nonetheless successful in some cases: visitors indeed found their fathers. One female visitor spoke with a newspaper reporter about her feelings on having seen her father in a photo that shows the execution of supposed partisans; he is watching the event with an evidently cheerful expression on his face. Now, she said, she understood better what her mother had told her about her father, who was missing in action in the Soviet Union. When he came home on leave from the front, he appeared increasingly changed to her, she no longer understood his reactions. Painfully then, but perhaps salubriously, a gap in this family's history was closed.

Most of the controversies arising about the exhibition were about photos, although it was much more than a photography exhibition. First and foremost, the exhibition presents texts: descriptions of events, the documentation of orders, letters from soldiers. The photos - many of which have been available for a long time in archives in the Federal Republic of Germany, others from recently opened archives in Moscow, Minsk, etc. - illustrate what the texts document. They do so - and this in part explains the disturbing effect the photos have had – from the soldiers' own perspective. The *Wehrmacht* soldiers photographed a great deal. For a variety of reasons, but why they do so cannot always be ascertained. Some of them surely wanted to document the events, conscious that these were crimes. Fascination may have lead others to photograph the bizarre and the cruel. Some of them, however - and the notes on the photos prove this - took pictures which they intended to carry and to take home with them as trophies. The exhibition forces the observer to see through the eyes of the witnesses, and thus sometimes through eyes that are watching what happens approvingly and with pleasure.

The authenticity of the photos has been called into question. They were said to be forgeries from archives in the Soviet Union. In no case was a charge of forgery made plausible, to say nothing of actual proof. There were long discussions of whether a given photo was correctly attributed to site A or whether it might not have been taken in the vicinity of B. (The fact is that it is no longer possible to establish the identity of specific photos with one hundred percent certainty when some have lain in wallets taken from prisoners of war for half a century. The fact is that certain photos can be found in more than one archive bearing different captions.) One photo[14] became the object of polemic attacks, because it appeared especially often in reports on the exhibition. The claims made were that the photo was a forgery, that the shooting depicted had been carried out by the (Waffen) SS and not by the Wehrmacht, that a regulation trial had preceded the execution, or that far fewer than 36 people had been executed. The debate went on until a witness attested to the authenticity of the photo. He had been present and was an especially credible witness because he still felt the execution had been justified - those shot were partisans and their execution was, in his opinion, legally correct.

Altogether, four main objections to the exhibition were raised: the crimes shown were, in fact, not crimes but rather acts of reprisal for partisan attacks and as such permitted by generally accepted martial law and by the Hague Convention on Land Warfare; the crimes acknowledged as such were committed by the SS, rather than the Wehrmacht; the exhibition generalizes by referring to "the Wehrmacht" when in fact only a minority of Wehrmacht members were involved in criminal acts; and, the final claim, the exhibition merely depicts occurrences which are part of every war.

The claim that the crimes shown were legitimate anti-partisan measures ignores the fact that the Wehrmacht waged a systematic war against partisans before any organized partisan movement existed. From the beginning, certain groups of people, in particular Jews, were defined as partisans and the murder of these people passed off as acts covered by

martial law and the rules of warfare. Apart from that, one must call to mind the words of Otto Schily quoted above. Those who do not hesitate to condone such anti-partisan measures as justified reveal, more than half a century after the end of the war, where their sympathies lie – in particular in those cases in which perhaps one or two odd photos may, coincidentally, show operations legitimated by the Hague Convention on Land Warfare[15].

The claim that only SS men were actively involved in these crimes has been refuted by historians, a fact which this exhibition aimed to document. Nevertheless, there have extensive debates about which crimes of the Wehrmacht were perpetrated in cooperation with the SS and the Einsatzgruppen (and about whether a photo didn't in fact prove that the Wehrmacht was not involved, merely because it showed an SS man standing next to a Wehrmacht officer). An integral component of the legend of the "unsullied Wehrmacht" was the contention that crimes which undisputedly did occur were committed solely by those wearing other uniforms and even proof of the contrary made no difference – what cannot be could not have happened. Understandably enough, this inner-German discussion unsettled people like Ignatz Bubis (the chairman of the National Council of Jews in Germany) and Andrzej Szczypiorski (the author of numerous novels on the Holocaust in Poland), who were among those who held public lectures when the exhibition was shown in various German cities. In their minds, what was important was not which uniforms the German criminals wore but rather the fact that they were Germans.

To focus on the crimes of the Wehrmacht is to focus on crimes in which, potentially, the normal German participated. What may seem an artificial differentiation to non-Germans or Jewish-Germans is a distinction which continues to reverberate throughout German society and awakens deep-seated emotions.

In speaking of "crimes of the Wehrmacht", one is neither claiming that all members of

this organization were personally involved in crimes, nor that all these members became criminals merely because of their (for the most part involuntary) membership in this organization. They did, however, belong to an organization that committed crimes - not by accident but systematically, not here and there but, in the Balkans and in various parts of the former Soviet Union, on a massive scale. These were crimes not only according to today's international norms but also from the perspective of contemporary international opinion. And these crimes were not the result of uncontrolled escalation or political pressure from civilian rulers, but were, from the outset, part of the military leadership's war plan.

Nevertheless - or perhaps for that very reason - the title of the exhibition was, from the beginning, the subject of perhaps the most heated debates. The German title – "War of Annihilation" – was chosen to emphasize that the exhibition was concerned with a special kind of war (the planning and the waging of war). The subtitle "Crimes of the Wehrmacht" was consciously placed in a subordinate position and was intended to direct attention to the legal categorization of this type of war. From the beginning, however, the media wrote about the "Wehrmacht exhibition". It made no difference that every visitor could clearly see that the exhibition was not about " the Wehrmacht" – the exhibition only dealt with three theaters of war in the East. A single phrase in the title – of the Wehrmacht – sufficed to "insult millions of German soldiers", "denigrate an entire generation" and so on. Absurd changes to the title were suggested, such as "Crimes in the Wehrmacht" (as if it were a matter of German soldiers murdering their fellow-soldiers) or "The involvement of individual soldiers of the Wehrmacht in crimes of the National Socialist State" (as if there were only isolated cases of passive involvement in crimes and as if Wehrmacht leaders in no case participated in planning and carrying out these crimes).

Besides the charges and claims presented above, another terse comment frequently made, with a shrug of the shoulders as it were, was simply "That's war". No doubt, only very rarely have wars taken place in which all sides did not commit war crimes – that is, killings and other atrocities which were not permissible according to the legal standards of the parties waging war – above and beyond the cruelties that are themselves war, because wars are undertakings in which human beings are forced to kill large numbers of other human beings. But the German *Wehrmacht*'s war of annihilation in the East was not a war with the aim of defeating an enemy army and then establishing an occupation regime. Instead, the war itself was part of a plan to exterminate part of the enemy population (the Jews) and enslave part of the remaining population. In contrast to the West and the North, no attempt was made to install satellite regimes, although this might have been feasible in White Russia and the Ukraine.

Interesting discussions arose when the exhibition was shown in various German and Austrian cities, in particular when former *Wehrmacht* soldiers were involved and the debates moved beyond the usual exchange of cliches. These discussions revealed how fundamentally veterans' memories of the war can differ. A confrontation at the exhibition venue in Stuttgart nearly ended in a fist-fight when a war veteran shouted "Lies" and "Slander" and a former fellow-soldier retorted: "What are you talking about, we saw all of that happen!" Some were only willing to talk about what they themselves had suffered in the war, the brutality of partisan warfare and other experiences. Some made statements like that of the veteran whose leg had been amputated, who, as he said, "had been part of it from the beginning", had lost his leg in the battle of Stalingrad and had been one of the last to be flown out: "We saw that, we did it. Everything in the exhibition is correct, down to the last dot."

It has taken more than half a century until German society was willing to confront its past as a National Socialist community, a *Volksgemeinschaft*. The success of two recently published books were signs of this willingness: first, Victor Klemper's diary,[16] the meticulous record of a Jewish survivor in a German city and second, the German translation of Daniel Goldhagen's book, "Hitler's Willing Executioners."[17] These successes were as unforeseen as that of the exhibition "War of Annihilation." Unforeseen, and yet, if one analyzes these events and their antecedents, they become explicable.

1. *Verhandlungen des Deutschen Bundestages, Stenographischer Bericht, Plenarprotokoll 13/163* (Bonn: Deutscher Bundestag, March 13, 1997), p. 14714.

2. *Verhandlungen des Deutschen Bundestages, Stenographischer Bericht, Plenarprotokoll 13/163* (Bonn: Deutscher Bundestag, March 13, 1997), p. 14718-14719.

3. *Verhandlungen des Deutschen Bundestages, Stenographischer Bericht, Plenarprotokoll 13/163* (Bonn: Deutscher Bundestag, March 13, 1997), p. 14719-14720.

4. Konrad Adenauer in a letter to Pastor Bernhard Custodis in Bonn, February 2, 1946 (letter 169) in: Konrad Adenauer (H.P. Mensing, ed.) *Briefe 1945-1946* (Berlin: Siedler, 1983), p. 172ff.

5. This is, to be sure, a question of one's personal willingness to feel sympathy with others. People in Germany were, of course, aware of the lawlessness, the violent attacks, the constant harassment, and the loss of opportunities which characterized daily life for Jews in Germany—before the systematic deportations began.

6. Gitta Sereny, *Albert Speer: His Battle with Truth* (New York: Alfred A. Knopf, 1995).

7. Hamburger Institut für Sozialforschung, ed., *Besucher einer Ausstellung* (Hamburg: Hamburger Edition, 1998), p.10.

8. International Military Tribunal, *Trial of the Major War Criminals before the International Military Tribunal, Nuremberg, 14 November 1945- 1 October 1946* (Nuremberg: International Military Tribunal, 1947), vol.1, pp. 278-279.

9. *Verhandlungen des Deutschen Bundestages, Stenographischer Bericht, 1: Wahlperiode* (Bonn: Deutscher Bundestag, 1949), vol. 6, p. 4983.

10. *Verhandlungen des Deutschen Bundestages, Stenographischer Bericht, 1: Wahlperiode* (Bonn: Deutscher Bundestag, 1949), vol. 6, pp. 4983-4984.

11. With varying degrees of intensity and varying consequences...

12. Although camps like Bergen-Belsen, Neuengamme, Dachau, Buchenwald, Sachsenhausen etc. were in the middle of Germany and the normal population was in fact aware of their existence, the death camps—Auschwitz, Treblinka, Belzec, Sobibor, Majdanek—were in Poland.

13. Little notice was taken of studies such as Raul Hilberg's investigation of the role of the *Reichsbahn*, the German railway company, in the Holocaust: Raul Hilberg, *The Role of the German Railroads in the Destruction of the Jews*, unpublished manuscript; German edition: Raul Hilberg, *Sonderzüge nach Auschwitz* (Mainz: Dumjahn, 1981).

14. See page 44, photo 3 in this volume. The photo shows a *Wehrmacht* soldier during the shooting of Serbian civilians in Pančevo.

15. Whether or not this might have been the case in isolated instances is something the photos do not reveal. However, the orders issued by the *Wehrmacht* make it quite clear that it was irrelevant whether or not the actual or so-called anti-partisan operations were legitimated by legal norms.

16. Victor Klemperer, (ed. by Walter Nowojski in cooperation with Christian Löser) *Ich will Zeugnis ablegen bis zum letzten. Tagebücher 1933-1945* (Berlin: Aufbau Verlag, 1996).

17. Daniel Goldhagen, *Hitler's Willing Executioners* (New York: Alfred A. Knopf, 1996). Goldhagen's book was the subject of controversy among historians in Germany and the US. In spite of that, Goldhagen, who toured Germany for a number of discussions, as well as his book were very successful in Germany. The success of these personal appearances can be attributed to the fact that he always began his talks with the following argument: Wherever genocide has taken place throughout the world, the assumption has been that those who planned and carried out such atrocities were convinced that genocide was necessary and morally justified. The question of how mass murder could take place, when no one (or only an extremely small minority) wanted it to happen, is one which is only posed in the case of the Holocaust. According to Goldhagen, this is absurd. The reaction of the audience was always the same: a kind of relieved sigh—"At last, someone has said what we have never even dared to really think."

# Glossary of German Terms Used in the Text

*Arbeitsjuden*
"Labor Jews", Jews compelled to do forced labor
by the Nazis

*artfremd*
alien, according to the Nazi race ideology of the
German *Volk* and its nature

*artverwandt*
racially related, according to the Nazi definition
of *Volk*

*Baden-Würtemberg*
a *Land* of the Federal Republic of Germany

*Dulag*
acronym for *Durchgangslager*, transit camp

*Einsatzgruppe*
mobile units, set up by SD head Heydrich for special
"tasks", e.g the extermination of Eastern European Jews

*Einsatzkommando*
task forces, subunits of the SS-*Einsatzgruppen*

*Flintenweib*
gun woman, contemptuous term for women soldiers
or other armed women

*Fremdvölker*
foreign peoples, Nazi term for all ethnic groups
defined as non-Aryan and racially not related to the
German *Volk*

*Generalgouvernement*
those parts of Polish territory which were occupied
and ruled by the Nazis from 1939 to 1945 but were not
annexed as part of the German Reich

*Großdeutschland Regiment*
name of a Wehrmacht regiment, later the name
of a division

*Hamsterfahrten*
"hamster trips", trips to the countryside undertaken
by civilians to procure food

*Hilfsvölker*
"auxilliary peoples", Nazi term for "inferior" races, seen
as fit only to serve the German *Volk*

*Judenräte*
Jewish councils, councils set up by Jewish communities by
order of the Nazis to carry out Nazi measures such as
resettlement in ghettos etc.

*Kreis*
administrative district of a *Land* in the Federal Republic
of Germany

*Land*
one of the federal states of the Federal Republic
of Germany

*Landeskriminalamt*
the Criminal Investigation Office of a *Land*

*Landgericht*
court of a *Land*

*Landser*
ordinary soldier, term roughly equivalent to G.I.

*Lebensraum*
living space, which the Nazis intended to capture
for the expansion of the German *Volk*

*Ministerialrat*
senior official in a ministry

*Nordrhein-Westfalen*
North Rhine – Westphalia, a *Land* of the Federal
Republic of Germany

*Ostland*
a Nazi civilian administrative entity including the
Baltic countries, parts of Poland and the western part
of Belorussia

*Reichsführer-SS*
head of the SS; Heinrich Himmler held this position
and was also Chief of the German Police

*Schutzstaffel*
Defense Squad of the Nazi Party

*Sonderkommando*
special task force, subunit of the *SS-Einsatzgruppen*

*Spieß*
colloquial term for a first sergeant, similar to "top kick"

*SS-Hauptsturmführer*
rank in the *Waffen-SS*, equivalent to captain

*SS-Brigadenführer*
rank in the *Waffen-SS*, equivalent to major-general

*SS-Oberscharführer*
rank in the *Waffen-SS*, equivalent to first sergeant

*SS-Obersturmführer*
rank in the *Waffen-SS*, equivalent to first lieutenant

*SS-Standartenführer*
rank in the *Waffen-SS*, equivalent to colonel

*Sturmabteilungen*
Storm Troops of the Nazi Party

*Untermensch*
subhuman creature, refers in Nazi jargon to a person
who belongs to an "inferior race"

*Untermenschentum*
sub-humanity, refers to peoples and ethnic groups
considered to be "inferior races"

*völkisch*
anything pertaining to the Nazi racial concept
of the German *Volk*

*Volkskrieg*
racial or people's war, fought to subjugate "inferior
races" under the rule of the German *Volk* and
to secure *Lebensraum*

*Volkstum*
refers to the German *Volk* and those ethnic groups
deemed closely related

*Waffen-SS*
Armed Forces of the SS

*Warthegau*
administrative area created in October 1939 and
including those parts of Polish territory which were
annexed by the Nazis as part of the German Reich

*Wehrmacht*
German Armed Forces

*Weltanschauung*
world view, ideology, or philosophy

*Weltanschauungskrieg*
war motivated by *Weltanschauung*, a world view,
ideology, or philosophy

# Abbreviations Used in German Documents

| Abbreviations | German term | English translation or equivalent |
|---|---|---|
| (Geb.)A.K. | (Gebirgs-)Armeekorps | (Mountain) Army Corps |
| A.H.Qu. | Armeehauptquartier | Army Headquarters |
| Abt. | Abteilung | batallion, detachment, unit, department, section |
| Abw. | Abwehr | defense, security, (counter- ) intelligence |
| AOK | Armee-Oberkommando | High Command of the Army |
| Art. | Artillerie | artillery |
| Az. | Aktenzeichen | file reference number |
| Bef., Befh. | Befehlshaber | commander |
| Bev., Bevollm. | Bevollmächtigter | Plenipotentiary |
| Btl. | Bataillon | batallion |
| Bttr(n). | Batterie(n) | battery (batteries) |
| Div. | Division | division |
| E.K. | Eisernes Kreuz | Iron Cross |
| f.d.R.d.A. | für die Richtigkeit der Angaben | statements confirmed by |
| geh. | geheim | secret, confidential |
| GFP | Geheime Feldpolizei | Secret Field Police |
| H.Dv. | Heeresdienstvorschrift | army regulations |
| Höh.Kdo | Höheres Kommando (Armeekorps) | higher command (army corps) |
| i. Genst. | im Generalstab | in the General Staff |
| i.A. | im Auftrag | by order of |
| I.R., J.R. | Infanterie-Regiment | infantry regiment |
| Ia | erster Generalstabsoffizier (Operationsabteilung) | First General Staff Officer (Operations Section) |
| Ic | dritter Generalstabsoffizier (Feindaufklärung) | Third General Staff Officer (Intelligence) |
| K.Z. | Konzentrationslager | concentration camp |
| Kdo. | Kommando (Armeekorps) | command (army corps) |
| Kdr. | Kommandeur, Kommandierender | commander, commanding officer |
| Kp., Kpn. | Kompanie, Kompanien | company, companies |
| KSSVO | Kriegssonderstrafrechtsverordnung | Military Anti-Sedition Law |
| KTB | Kriegstagebuch | War Journal |
| LKW | Lastkraftwagen | truck |
| Lt. | Leutnant | second lieutenant |
| M.G., MG | Maschinengewehr | machine gun |
| Mil.V. | Militärverwaltung | military administration |
| NSV, N.S.V. | Nationalsozialistische Volkswohlfahrt | National Socialist People's Welfare |
| O.U. | Ortsunterkunft | local billet, local quarters |
| Off., Offz. | Offizier | officer |
| OKH | Oberkommando des Heeres | High Command of the Army |
| OKW | Oberkommando der Wehrmacht | High Command of the Armed Forces |
| O.Q. | Oberquartiermeister | General Staff Supply and Administration Officer (at Army or Army Group level) |
| Ord. | Ordonnanz | orderly |
| PK | Propagandakompanie | Propaganda Company |
| Q. | Quartiermeister | corps or division quartermaster |
| Res.Pol.Btln. | Reserve-Polizeibataillon | Reserve Police Batallion |
| RSHA | Reichssicherheitshauptamt | Reich Security Main Office |
| SD | Sicherheitsdienst | Security Service, secret police of the SS |
| SK | Sonderkommando | special task force, subunits of the SS Einsatzgruppen |
| SS | Schutzstaffel | Defense Squad, Nazi Party elite guard |
| Verw. | Verwaltung | administration |
| z.b.V. | zur besonderen Verwendung | for special duty |

# Further Reading

Anderson, Truman O. (1995), "Die 62. Infanterie-Division. Repressalien im Heeresgebiet Süd, Oktober bis Dezember 1941," in Hannes Heer and Klaus Naumann (eds.) *Vernichtungskrieg. Verbrechen der Wehrmacht 1941 bis 1944*, Hamburg, pp. 297-314. *

Anderson, Truman O. (1995), *The conduct of reprisals by the German army of occupation in the southern USSR*, UMI Diss. Services, Ann Arbor, Mich.-Chicago, Illinois, Univ. of Chicago.

Bartov, Omer (1992), *Hitler's Army. Soldiers, Nazis and War in the Third Reich*, Oxford.

Boog, Horst, et al. (1983), *Der Angriff auf die Sowjetunion, Stuttgart, (Das Deutsche Reich und der Zweite Weltkrieg*, vol. 4).

Boll, Bernd and Safrian, Hans (1995), "Auf dem Weg nach Stalingrad. Die 6. Armee 1941/42," in Hannes Heer and Klaus Naumann (eds.) *Vernichtungskrieg. Verbrechen der Wehrmacht 1941 bis 1944*, Hamburg, pp. 260-296. *

Browning, Christopher (1993), *Ordinary Men: Reserve Police Battalion 101 and the Final Solution in Poland*, New York.

Chiari, Bernhard (1998), *Alltag hinter der Front. Besatzung, Kollaboration und Widerstand in Weißrußland 1941-1944*, Düsseldorf.

Hamburger Institut für Sozialforschung (ed.) (1999), *Eine Ausstellung und ihre Folgen. Zur Rezeption der Ausstellung „Vernichtungskrieg. Verbrechen der Wehrmacht 1941 bis 1944"*, Hamburg.

— (ed.) (1998), *Besucher einer Ausstellung. Die Ausstellung „Vernichtungskrieg. Verbrechen der Wehrmacht 1941 bis 1944" in Interview und Gespräch*, Hamburg.

— (ed.) (1998), *Krieg ist ein Gesellschaftszustand. Reden zur Eröffnung der Ausstellung Vernichtungskrieg. Verbrechen der Wehrmacht 1941 bis 1944"*, Hamburg.

Heer, Hannes and Naumann, Klaus (eds.) (1995), *Vernichtungskrieg. Verbrechen der Wehrmacht 1941 bis 1944*, Hamburg. *

Heer, Hannes (1995), "Killing Fields. Die Wehrmacht und der Holocaust", in Hannes Heer and Klaus Naumann (eds.) *Vernichtungskrieg. Verbrechen der Wehrmacht 1941 bis 1944*, Hamburg, pp. 57-77. *

Heer, Hannes (1995), "Die Logik des Vernichtungskrieges. Wehrmacht und Partisanenkampf", in Hannes Heer and Klaus Naumann (eds.) *Vernichtungskrieg. Verbrechen der Wehrmacht 1941 bis 1944*, Hamburg, pp. 104-138. *

— (ed.) (1995), *"Stets zu erschiessen sind Frauen, die in der Roten Armee dienen." Geständnisse deutscher Kriegsgefangener über ihren Einsatz an der Ostfront*, Hamburg.

Hilberg, Raul (1985), *The Destruction of the European Jews*, New York.

Krausnick, Helmut (1989), *Hitlers Einsatzgruppen: die Truppe des Weltanschauungskrieges 1938-1942*, Frankfurt/M.

Latzel, Klaus (1998), *Deutsche Soldaten – nationalsozialistischer Krieg? Kriegserlebnis – Kriegserfahrung 1939-1944*, Hamburg.

Manoschek, Walter (ed.) (1995), *"Es gibt nur eines für das Judentum: Vernichtung." Das Judenbild in deutschen Soldatenbriefen 1939-1944*, Hamburg.

Manoschek, Walter (1995), "'Gehst mit Juden erschiessen?' Die Vernichtung der Juden in Serbien," in Hannes Heer and Klaus Naumann (eds.) *Vernichtungskrieg. Verbrechen der Wehrmacht 1941 bis 1944*, Hamburg, pp. 104-138. *

— (1993), *"Serbien ist judenfrei": militärische Besatzungspolitik und Judenvernichtung in Serbien 1941/42*, München.

Müller, Rolf-Dieter (1991), *Hitlers Ostkrieg und die deutsche Siedlungspolitik. Die Zusammenarbeit von Wehrmacht, Wirtschaft und SS*, Frankfurt/M.

Müller, Rolf-Dieter and Gerd R. Ueberschär (1997), *Hitlers War in the East. 1941-1945: a critical assessment*, New York.

Rosenberg, Heinz (1992), *Jahre des Schreckens*, Göttingen.

Rössler, Mechthild, et al. (eds.) (1993), *Der "Generalplan Ost": Hauptlinien der nationalsozialistischen Planungs- und Vernichtungspolitik*, Berlin.

Sommer, Theo (ed.) (1995), *Gehorsam bis zum Mord? Der verschwiegene Krieg der deutschen Wehrmacht — Fakten, Analysen, Debatte, Zeit-Punkte*, Heft 3, Hamburg.

Streit, Christian (1991), *Keine Kameraden: die Wehrmacht und die sowjetischen Kriegsgefangenen 1941-1945*, Bonn.

Ueberschär, Gerd R. (ed.) (2000), *Der militärische Widerstand und seine Haltung zu den NS Verbrechen*, Darmstadt.

Ueberschär, Gerd R. (ed.) (1998), *Hitlers militärische Elite*, Darmstadt.

Ueberschär, Gerd R./ Wette, Wolfram (1984), *Unternehmen "Barbarossa": der deutsche Überfall auf die Sowjetunion 1941. Berichte, Analysen, Dokumente*, Paderborn.

* A U.S. edition of this volume is scheduled for publication in late 1999.

# Photographic Credits

| | | |
|---|---|---|
| 24 | 1 | Main Comission for the Investigation of Crimes against the Polish Nation, Warsaw |
| 24 | 2 | Main Comission for the Investigation of Crimes against the Polish Nation, Warsaw |
| 24 | 3 | Main Comission for the Investigation of Crimes against the Polish Nation, Warsaw |
| 25 | 4 | Main Comission for the Investigation of Crimes against the Polish Nation, Warsaw |
| 25 | 5 | Main Comission for the Investigation of Crimes against the Polish Nation, Warsaw |
| 25 | 6 | Main Comission for the Investigation of Crimes against the Polish Nation, Warsaw |
| 26 | 1 | Main Comission for the Investigation of Crimes against the Polish Nation, Warsaw |
| 26 | 2 | Main Comission for the Investigation of Crimes against the Polish Nation, Warsaw |
| 27 | 3 | Main Comission for the Investigation of Crimes against the Polish Nation, Warsaw |
| 27 | 4 | Main Comission for the Investigation of Crimes against the Polish Nation, Warsaw |
| 27 | 5 | Main Comission for the Investigation of Crimes against the Polish Nation, Warsaw |
| 27 | 6 | Main Comission for the Investigation of Crimes against the Polish Nation, Warsaw |
| 27 | 7 | Main Comission for the Investigation of Crimes against the Polish Nation, Warsaw |
| 27 | 8 | Main Comission for the Investigation of Crimes against the Polish Nation, Warsaw |
| 27 | 9 | Main Comission for the Investigation of Crimes against the Polish Nation, Warsaw |
| 27 | 10 | Main Comission for the Investigation of Crimes against the Polish Nation, Warsaw |
| 37 | 1 | Bundesarchiv Koblenz, Photograph 141/ 1005 |
| 37 | 2 | Jewish Museum, Belgrade |
| 37 | 3 | Bundesarchiv Koblenz, Photograph 122/ 16226/ 20a |
| 40 | 2 | Bundesarchiv Koblenz, Photograph 101/ 185/ 112/ 9 |
| 40 | 3 | Bundesarchiv Koblenz, Photograph 101/ 185/ 112/ 4 |
| 40 | 4 | Bundesarchiv Koblenz, Photograph 101/ 185/ 112/ 13 |
| 40 | 5 | Bundesarchiv Koblenz, Photograph 101/ 185/ 112/ 38 |
| 41 | 6 | Museum of the Revolution, Belgrade |
| 41 | 7 | Jewish Museum, Belgrade |
| 41 | 8 | Jewish Museum, Belgrade |
| 42 | 1 | Deutsches Historisches Museum, Berlin/ Bildarchiv Gronefeld |
| 43 | 2 | Deutsches Historisches Museum, Berlin/ Bildarchiv Gronefeld |
| 43 | 3 | Deutsches Historisches Museum, Berlin/ Bildarchiv Gronefeld |
| 43 | 4 | Deutsches Historisches Museum, Berlin/ Bildarchiv Gronefeld |
| 44 | 1 | Deutsches Historisches Museum, Berlin/ Bildarchiv Gronefeld |
| 44 | 2 | Deutsches Historisches Museum, Berlin/ Bildarchiv Gronefeld |
| 44 | 3 | Deutsches Historisches Museum, Berlin/ Bildarchiv Gronefeld |
| 45 | 4 | Deutsches Historisches Museum, Berlin/ Bildarchiv Gronefeld |
| 47 | 1 | Yugoslavian Archive, Belgrade |
| 47 | 2 | Yugoslavian Archive, Belgrade |
| 48 | 1 | Museum of the Revolution, Belgrade |
| 48 | 2 | Museum of the Revolution, Belgrade |
| 48 | 3 | Museum of the Revolution, Belgrade |
| 49 | 4 | Museum of the Revolution, Belgrade |
| 49 | 5 | Museum of the Revolution, Belgrade |
| 49 | 6 | Museum of the Revolution, Belgrade |
| 50 | 1 | Yugoslavian Archive, Belgrade |
| 50 | 2 | Yugoslavian Archive, Belgrade |
| 50 | 3 | Museum of the Revolution, Belgrade |
| 51 | 4 | Yugoslavian Archive, Belgrade |
| 51 | 5 | Jewish Museum, Belgrade |
| 51 | 6 | Museum of the Revolution, Belgrade |
| 51 | 7 | Jewish Museum, Belgrade |
| 53 | 1 | Museum of the Revolution, Belgrade |
| 53 | 2 | Museum of the Revolution, Belgrade |
| 53 | 3 | Military Museum, Belgrade |
| 54 | 1 | Museum of the Revolution, Belgrade |
| 55 | 2 | Military Museum, Belgrade |
| 55 | 3 | Military Museum, Belgrade |
| 55 | 4 | Military Museum, Belgrade |
| 55 | 5 | Military Museum, Belgrade |
| 55 | 6 | Military Museum, Belgrade |
| 56 | 1 | Yugoslavian Archive, Belgrade |
| 56 | 2 | Military Museum, Belgrade |
| 56 | 3 | Military Museum, Belgrade |
| 57 | 4 | Military Museum, Belgrade |
| 57 | 5 | Military Museum, Belgrade |
| 57 | 6 | Yugoslavian Archive, Belgrade |
| 58 | 1 | Military Museum, Belgrade |
| 58 | 2 | Yugoslavian Archive, Belgrade |
| 58 | 3 | Military Museum, Belgrade |
| 59 | 4 | Military Museum, Belgrade |
| 59 | 5 | Jewish Museum, Belgrade |
| 59 | 6 | Military Museum, Belgrade |
| 59 | 7 | Military Museum, Belgrade |
| 63 | 1 | _sterreichisches Staatsarchiv |
| 63 | 2 | _sterreichisches Staatsarchiv |
| 63 | 3 | _sterreichisches Staatsarchiv |
| 63 | 4 | _sterreichische Nationalbibliothek |
| 63 | 5 | _sterreichische Nationalbibliothek |
| 65 | 1 | Military Museum, Belgrade |
| 65 | 2 | Military Museum, Belgrade |
| 65 | 3 | Military Museum, Belgrade |
| 65 | 4 | Military Museum, Belgrade |
| 66 | 1 | Military Museum, Belgrade |
| 66 | 2 | Military Museum, Belgrade |
| 67 | 3 | Military Museum, Belgrade |
| 67 | 4 | Military Museum, Belgrade |
| 67 | 5 | Hessisches Hauptstaatsarchiv, Wiesbaden |
| 70 | 1 | Museum of the Revolution, Belgrade |
| 70 | 2 | Museum of the Revolution, Belgrade |
| 70 | 3 | Military Museum, Belgrade |
| 71 | 4 | Museum of the Revolution, Belgrade |
| 71 | 5 | Museum of the Revolution, Belgrade |
| 71 | 6 | Museum of the Revolution, Belgrade |
| 71 | 7 | Museum of the Revolution, Belgrade |
| 71 | 8 | Museum of the Revolution, Belgrade |
| 74 | | Memorial Kragujevac |
| 75 | | Memorial Kragujevac |
| 80 | 1 | Bundesarchiv Koblenz, Photograph 101/ 187/ 203/ 2a |
| 80 | 2 | Bundesarchiv Koblenz, Photograph 101/ 187/ 203/ 6a |
| 80 | 4 | Bundesarchiv Koblenz, Photograph 101/ 187/ 202/ 15a |
| 81 | 3 | Bundesarchiv Koblenz, Photograph 101/ 187/ 202/ 23 |
| 81 | 5 | Bundesarchiv Koblenz, Photograph 101/ 187/ 203/ 9 |
| 81 | 6 | Bundesarchiv Koblenz, Photograph 101/ 187/ 203/ 28a |
| 81 | 7 | Bundesarchiv Koblenz, Photograph 101/ 187/ 203/ 37a |
| 83 | 1 | Dokumentationsarchiv des Österreichischen Widerstands, Wien |
| 83 | 2 | Dokumentationsarchiv des Österreichischen Widerstands, Wien |
| 83 | 3 | Dokumentationsarchiv des Österreichischen Widerstands, Wien |
| 83 | 4 | Dokumentationsarchiv des Österreichischen Widerstands, Wien |
| 84 | 1 | Eva Better-Heitner, courtesy of United States Holocaust Memorial Museum, Washington D.C. |
| 85 | 2 | War History Archive, Prague |
| 85 | 3 | Jewish Historical Institute, courtesy of United States Holocaust Memorial Museum, Washington D.C. |
| 85 | 4 | Main Commission for the Investigation of Nazi War Crimes, courtesy of United States Holocaust Memorial Museum, Washington D.C. |
| 85 | 5 | Eva Better-Heitner, courtesy of United States Holocaust Memorial Museum, Washington D.C. |
| 85 | 6 | Main Commission for the Investigation of Nazi War Crimes, courtesy of United States Holocaust Memorial Museum, Washington D.C. |
| 87 | 1 | War History Archive, Prague |
| 87 | 2 | Yad Vashem, Jerusalem |
| 91 | 1 | Ukrainian Historical Museum, Kharkov |
| 91 | 2 | Zentrale Stelle der Landesjustizverwaltungen zur Aufklärung nationalsozialistischer Verbrechen, Ludwigsburg |
| 91 | 3 | Zentrale Stelle der Landesjustizverwaltungen zur Aufklärung nationalsozialistischer Verbrechen, Ludwigsburg |
| 91 | 4 | Zentrale Stelle der Landesjustizverwaltungen zur Aufklärung nationalsozialistischer Verbrechen, Ludwigsburg |
| 92 | 1 | Hessisches Hauptstaatsarchiv, Wiesbaden |
| 92 | 2 | Hessisches Hauptstaatsarchiv, Wiesbaden |
| 93 | 3 | Hessisches Hauptstaatsarchiv, Wiesbaden |
| 93 | 4 | Hessisches Hauptstaatsarchiv, Wiesbaden |
| 93 | 5 | Hessisches Hauptstaatsarchiv, Wiesbaden |
| 93 | 6 | Hessisches Hauptstaatsarchiv, Wiesbaden |
| 93 | 7 | Hessisches Hauptstaatsarchiv, Wiesbaden |

143 4 Private collection
143 5 Museum of the Great War of the Fatherland, Minsk
144 1 Bundesarchiv Koblenz, Photograph 101/ 267/ 111/ 36a
144 2 Bundesarchiv Koblenz, Photograph 101/ 267/ 111/ 38a
145 3 Museum of the Great War of the Fatherland, Minsk
145 4 Museum of the Great War of the Fatherland, Minsk
145 5 Private collection
145 6 Private collection
145 7 Private collection
145 8 Museum of the Great War of the Fatherland, Minsk
146 1 Museum of the Great War of the Fatherland, Minsk
146 2 Museum of the Great War of the Fatherland, Minsk
146 3 Museum of the Great War of the Fatherland, Minsk
146 4 Belorussian Archive for Film and Photographic Documents, Dzerzhinsk
147 5 Museum of the Great War of the Fatherland, Minsk
147 6 Museum of the Great War of the Fatherland, Minsk
147 7 Museum of the Great War of the Fatherland, Minsk
147 8 Museum of the Great War of the Fatherland, Minsk
147 9 Belorussian State Archive, Minsk
149 1 Museum of the Great War of the Fatherland, Minsk
149 2 Belorussian Archive for Film and Photographic Documents, Dzerzhinsk
149 3 Belorussian Archive for Film and Photographic Documents, Dzerzhinsk
149 4 Museum of the Great War of the Fatherland, Minsk
149 5 Belorussian Archive for Film and Photographic Documents, Dzerzhinsk
150 1 Private collection
150 2 Private collection
150 3 Private collection
150 7 Private collection
150 8 Private collection
150 12 Private collection
150 13 Private collection
151 4 Private collection
151 5 Private collection
151 6 Private collection
151 9 Private collection
151 10 Private collection
151 11 Private collection
151 14 Private collection
151 15 Private collection
151 16 Private collection
154 1 Bundesarchiv Koblenz, Photograph 3 (89/38/36)
154 2 Bundesarchiv Koblenz, Photograph 3 (89/38/35)
154 3 Bundesarchiv Koblenz, Photograph 3 (94/92/19a)
155 4 Belorussian Archive for Film and Photographic Documents, Dzerzhinsk
155 5 Belorussian Archive for Film and Photographic Documents, Dzerzhinsk
155 6 Belorussian Archive for Film and Photographic Documents, Dzerzhinsk

156 1 Museum of the Great War of the Fatherland, Minsk
156 2 Belorussian Archive for Film and Photographic Documents, Dzerzhinsk
157 3 Belorussian Archive for Film and Photographic Documents, Dzerzhinsk
157 4 Belorussian Archive for Film and Photographic Documents, Dzerzhinsk
157 5 Museum of the Great War of the Fatherland, Minsk
157 6 Museum of the Great War of the Fatherland, Minsk
157 7 Belorussian Archive for Film and Photographic Documents, Dzerzhinsk
157 8 Belorussian Archive for Film and Photographic Documents, Dzerzhinsk
158 1 Museum of the Great War of the Fatherland, Minsk
158 2 Bundesarchiv Koblenz, Photograph 3 (72/26/43)
159 3 Museum of the Great War of the Fatherland, Minsk
159 4 Museum of the Great War of the Fatherland, Minsk
159 5 Museum of the Great War of the Fatherland, Minsk
159 6 Bundesarchiv Koblenz, Photograph 3 (70/43/30)
159 7 Museum of the Great War of the Fatherland, Minsk
160 1 Bundesarchiv Koblenz, Photograph 101/ 286/ 811/ 19a
160 2 Bundesarchiv Koblenz, Photograph 101/ 286/ 815/ 2
160 3 Bundesarchiv Koblenz, Photograph 101/ 286/ 811/ 27a
160 6 Bundesarchiv Koblenz, Photograph 101/ 286/ 813/ 9
160 7 Bundesarchiv Koblenz, Photograph 101/ 286/ 813/ 15
160 8 Bundesarchiv Koblenz, Photograph 101/ 286/ 813/ 14
161 1 Belorussian Archive for Film and Photographic Documents, Dzerzhinsk
161 2 Belorussian Archive for Film and Photographic Documents, Dzerzhinsk
161 3 Museum of the Great War of the Fatherland, Minsk
161 4 Belorussian Archive for Film and Photographic Documents, Dzerzhinsk
161 4 Bundesarchiv Koblenz, Photograph 101/ 286/ 815/ 13
161 5 Bundesarchiv Koblenz, Photograph 101/ 286/ 815/ 25a
161 5 Russian State Archive for Film and Photographic Documents, Krasnogorsk
161 9 Bundesarchiv Koblenz, Photograph 101/ 286/ 813/ 18
161 10 Bundesarchiv Koblenz, Photograph 101/ 286/ 813/ 32
161 11 Bundesarchiv Koblenz, Photograph 101/ 286/ 813/ 34
161 12 Bundesarchiv Koblenz, Photograph 101/ 286/ 813/ 36
161 13 Bundesarchiv Koblenz, Photograph 101/ 286/ 813/ 37
164 1 Museum of the Great War of the Fatherland, Minsk
165 2 Museum of the Great War of the Fatherland, Minsk
165 3 Belorussian Archive for Film and Photographic Documents, Dzerzhinsk

165 4 Museum of the Great War of the Fatherland, Minsk
166 1 Bundesarchiv/ Militärarchiv Freiburg im Breisgau, RH 22/ 233
167 2 Belorussian Archive for Film and Photographic Documents, Dzerzhinsk
167 3 Belorussian Archive for Film and Photographic Documents, Dzerzhinsk
167 4 Belorussian Archive for Film and Photographic Documents, Dzerzhinsk
167 5 Museum of the Great War of the Fatherland, Minsk
167 6 Museum of the Great War of the Fatherland, Minsk
169 1 Belorussian Archive for Film and Photographic Documents, Dzerzhinsk
169 2 Belorussian Archive for Film and Photographic Documents, Dzerzhinsk
169 3 Belorussian Archive for Film and Photographic Documents, Dzerzhinsk
170 1 Belorussian Archive for Film and Photographic Documents, Dzerzhinsk
171 2 Russian State Archive for Film and Photographic Documents, Krasnogorsk
171 3 Russian State Archive for Film and Photographic Documents, Krasnogorsk
171 4 Russian State Archive for Film and Photographic Documents, Krasnogorsk
171 5 Belorussian Archive for Film and Photographic Documents, Dzerzhinsk
171 6 Museum of the Great War of the Fatherland, Minsk
173 1 Yad Vashem, Jerusalem
173 2 Yad Vashem, Jerusalem
173 3 Bundesarchiv Koblenz, Photograph 101/ 1/ 251/ 34
173 4 Main Commission for the Investigation of Nazi War Crimes, courtesy of United States Holocaust Memorial Museum, Washington D.C.
173 5 Main Commission for the Investigation of Nazi war Crimes, courtesy of United States Holocaust Memorial Museum, Washington D.C.
173 6 Bundesarchiv Koblenz, Photograph 101/ 270/ 298/ 6
173 7 Bundesarchiv Koblenz, Photograph 3 (94/27/36)
173 8 Bundesarchiv Koblenz, Photograph 3 (94/27/34)
173 9 YIVO-Institute for Jewish Research, New York
174 10 Yad Vashem, Jerusalem
174 11 Yad Vashem, Jerusalem
174 12 Yad Vashem, Jerusalem
174 13 Dokumentationsarchiv des Österreichischen Widerstands, Wien
174 14 Yad Vashem, Jerusalem
174 15 Yad Vashem, Jerusalem
174 16 Bundesarchiv Koblenz, Photograph 3 (94/27/33)
174 17 Bundesarchiv Koblenz, Photograph 3 (91/14/8)
174 18 National Archives, courtesy of United States Holocaust Memorial Museum, Washington D.C.
175 19 Dokumentationsarchiv des Österreichischen Widerstands, Wien
175 20 Dokumentationsarchiv des Österreichischen Widerstands, Wien
175 21 Dokumentationsarchiv des Österreichischen Widerstands, Wien

202 16 GARF-State Archives of the Russian Federation, Moscow

202 17 Bundesarchiv Koblenz, Photograph 101/ 267/ 111/ 9

202 18 Bundesarchiv Koblenz, Photograph 101/ 605/ 1721/ 3a

203 19 GARF-State Archives of the Russian Federation, Moscow

203 20 GARF-State Archives of the Russian Federation, Moscow

203 21 Dokumentationsarchiv des Österreichischen Widerstands, Wien

203 22 Belorussian Archive for Film and Photographic Documents, Dzerzhinsk

203 23 GARF-State Archives of the Russian Federation, Moscow

203 24 GARF-State Archives of the Russian Federation, Moscow

204 1 Museum of the Revolution, Belgrade, courtesy of United States Holocaust Memorial Museum, Washington D.C.

204 2 Belorussian Archive for Film and Photographic Documents, Dzerzhinsk

204 3 Museum of the Revolution, Belgrade, courtesy of United States Holocaust Memorial Museum, Washington D.C.

204 4 Belorussian Archive for Film and Photographic Documents, Dzerzhinsk

204 5 Russian State Archive for Film and Photographic Documents, Krasnogorsk

204 6 Russian State Archive for Film and Photographic Documents, Krasnogorsk

204 7 Russian State Archive for Film and Photographic Documents, Krasnogorsk

204 8 Russian State Archive for Film and Photographic Documents, Krasnogorsk

204 9 Museum of the Great War of the Fatherland, Minsk

205 10 Russian State Archive for Film and Photographic Documents, Krasnogorsk

205 11 Museum of the Great War of the Fatherland, Minsk

205 12 Russian State Archive for Film and Photographic Documents, Krasnogorsk

205 13 Russian State Archive for Film and Photographic Documents, Krasnogorsk

205 14 Russian State Archive for Film and Photographic Documents, Krasnogorsk

205 15 Bundesarchiv Koblenz, Photograph 122/ 16197/ 18

205 16 Russian State Archive for Film and Photographic Documents, Krasnogorsk

205 17 Russian State Archive for Film and Photographic Documents, Krasnogorsk

205 18 Russian State Archive for Film and Photographic Documents, Krasnogorsk

206 19 Belorussian Archive for Film and Photographic Documents, Dzerzhinsk

206 20 Belorussian Archive for Film and Photographic Documents, Dzerzhinsk

206 21 Russian State Archive for Film and Photographic Documents, Krasnogorsk

206 22 Russian State Archive for Film and Photographic Documents, Krasnogorsk

206 23 United States Holocaust Memorial Museum, Washington D.C., Ufficio Storico, Stato Maggiore dell' Esercito Italiano

206 24 United States Holocaust Memorial Museum, Washington D.C., Ufficio Storico, Stato Maggiore dell' Esercito Italiano

206 25 United States Holocaust Memorial Museum, Washington D.C., Ufficio Storico, Stato Maggiore dell' Esercito Italiano

206 26 Museum of the Great War of the Fatherland, Minsk

206 27 Private collection

207 28 Private collection

207 29 Private collection

207 30 Private collection

207 31 Private collection

207 32 Private collection

207 33 Russian State Archive for Film and Photographic Documents, Krasnogorsk

207 34 Russian State Archive for Film and Photographic Documents, Krasnogorsk

207 35 Russian State Archive for Film and Photographic Documents, Krasnogorsk

207 36 Russian State Archive for Film and Photographic Documents, Krasnogorsk

208 37 Museum of the Revolution, Belgrade, courtesy of United States Holocaust Memorial Museum, Washington D.C.

208 38 Museum of the Revolution, Belgrade, courtesy of United States Holocaust Memorial Museum, Washington D.C.

208 39 Russian State Archive for Film and Photographic Documents, Krasnogorsk

# Contributors

**Dr. Bernd Boll** is a historian. A research associate at the Hamburg Institute for Social Research, he is a member of the project group which produced and continues to accompany the exhibition "Vernichtungskrieg. Verbrechen der Wehrmacht 1941 bis 1944".

Publications:

(1993) *"Das wird man nie mehr los." Ausländische Zwangsarbeiter in der Offenburger Kriegswirtschaft 1939-1945*, Pfaffenweiler.

(1998) "Generalfeldmarschall Walther von Reichenau", in: Gerd R. Ueberschär (ed.), *Hitlers militärische Elite*, Vol. 1, Darmstadt, pp. 195-202.

(1998) "Generalfeldmarschall Erich von Lewinski, gen. von Mainstein", in Gerd R. Ueberschär (ed.), *Hitlers militärische Elite*, Vol. 2, Darmstadt, pp. 143-152

(1998) Wehrmacht vor Gericht, "Kriegsverbrecherprozesse der Vier Mächte nach 1945", in *Geschichte und Gesellschaft* 28, pp. 970-994.

Various contributions on the history of National Socialism and topics in cultural history in academic journals, collected volumes, and newspapers.

**Hannes Heer** is a historian and film maker. A research associate at the Hamburg Institute for Social Research, he is director of the project group which produced and continues to accompany the exhibition "Vernichtungskrieg. Verbrechen der Wehrmacht 1941 bis 1944".

Publications:

(1971), *Burgfrieden oder Klassenkampf. Zur Politik der sozialdemokratischen Gewerkschaften 1930-1933*, Neuwied.

(1975) *Ernst Thälmann*, Reinbek.

(ed.) (1983), *"Als ich 9 Jahre alt war, kam der Krieg"*, Reinbek.

(with Klaus Naumann, eds.) (1995), *Vernichtungskrieg. Verbrechen der Wehrmacht 1941 bis 1944*, Hamburg.

(ed.) (1995), *"Stets zu erschiessen sind Frauen, die in der Roten Armee dienen". Geständnisse deutscher Kriegsgefangener über ihren Einsatz an der Ostfront*, Hamburg.

(ed.) (1997), *Im Herzen der Finsternis. Victor Klemperer als Chronist der NS-Zeit*, Berlin.

(1999), *Die Deutsche Wehrmacht an der Ostfront*, Hamburg.

**Dr. Walter Manoschek** is a political scientist and a lecturer and researcher at the Institut für Staats- und Politikwissenschaft of the University of Vienna. As a research associate at the Hamburg Institute for Social Research, he is a member of the project group which produced the exhibition "Vernichtungskrieg. Verbrechen der Wehrmacht 1941 bis 1944"; in particular, he was responsible for accompanying the exhibition at presentations in Austria.

Publications:

(1993), *"Serbien ist judenfrei." Militärische Besatzungspolitik und Judenvernichtung in Serbien 1941/42*, Munich.

(with Gabriele Anderl) (1993), *Gescheiterte Flucht. Das Schicksal des jüdischen Kladovo-Transportes auf dem Weg nach Palästina 1939-1942*, Vienna.

(ed.) (1995), *"Es gibt nur eines für das Judentum: Vernichtung". Das Judenbild in deutschen Soldatenbriefen 1939-1944*, Hamburg.

**Dr. Hans Safrian** is a historian. He is a member of the project group which produced the exhibition Vernichtungskrieg. Verbrechen der Wehrmacht 1941 bis 1944.

Publication:

(1993), *Die Eichmann-Männer*, Vienna/Zurich.

**Christian Reuther** has conceived and designed exhibitions since 1990. He is a member of the project group which produced the exhibition "Vernichtungskrieg. Verbrechen der Wehrmacht 1941 bis 1944".

Exhibitions:

"Nichts mehr zu sagen und nichts zu beweinen. Ein jüdischer Friedhof in Deutschland," shown at the Museum für Sepulkralkultur Kassel, Museum Bochum, Deutsches Historisches Museum Berlin, Europäisches Kulturzentrum Erfurt;

"Vernichtungskrieg. Verbrechen der Wehrmacht 1941 bis 1944";

"Reisst auch der letzte Faden. Jüdische Schulen," in the Jüdisches Museum in the Stadtmuseum, Martin-Gropius-Bau Berlin.

Publication:

(1994), *"Nichts mehr zu sagen und nichts zu beweinen". Lehrstücke und Lesarten zu einem jüdischen Friedhof*, Berlin.